Characters of North

Compiled by Raymond Monbiot

Published in 2003 by:
Rotherfield Management Ltd
Eastgate House
Overy Road
Burnham Market
Norfolk
PE31 8HH

© Raymond Monbiot

ISBN 0 9542567 1 9

All rights reserved. No part of this publication may be reproduced, stored in a retrieval system, or transmitted in any form or by any means, electronic, mechanical, photocopying, recording, or otherwise, without prior permission of the publisher.

Typesetting:
Raymond Monbiot

Printed by:
BARNWELL'S OF AYLSHAM
Penfold Street,
Aylsham, Norfolk
NR11 6ET

CONTENTS   Page

Foreword	4
About the Author	7

The Burnhams

Burnham Overy
1.	Leslie and Betty Harvey	11
2.	June Dye	21

Burnham Thorpe
3.	Beryl Alexander	29

Burnham Market
4.	Reg Mussett	39
5.	Diana Mansell	47
6.	Jimmy Rout	61
7.	Peter Groom	69
8.	Annie Franklin	75
9.	Ivy Wells	81

Dersingham
10.	Ray Scoles	89

Swaffham and Burnham Market
11.	Mary Tuck	97

Wells next the Sea
12.	Arthur Howell	105

Foreword

In 1966 a woman aged 106 recalled the account of the Battle of Waterloo, as told her by her grandfather, who fought in the Duke of Wellington's army in 1815. On the morning after the battle the field was white - the last sight one would have imagined but it was the result of the cotton wads of the cartridges lying thick upon the ground.

This kindled my interest in living history. The characters in this, my second book in this series (the first is *The Burnhams Book of Characters and Memories),* have lived in North Norfolk for most, if not all, of their lives. Their memories and stories date back in some cases over 80 years. However these have rarely been committed to paper and there was a danger that they would be lost forever.

This book is about real people who have lived and worked in North Norfolk through good times and bad. Jimmy Rout is one of the last surviving prisoners of war of the Japanese, Ray Scoles is butcher by Royal Appointment to Sandringham House, Beryl Alexander was for 43 years housekeeper to Lord and Lady Zuckerman at the Shooting Box in Burnham Thorpe, Mary Tuck is a relative of Howard Carter who, with Lord Carnarvon, found Tutankhamun's tomb. These are just five examples of 12 compelling chapters.

There was severe hardship in North Norfolk in the 1920s and 30s when the struggle to raise a family and make ends meet, with no state help, meant the larger the family the poorer they tended to be. Feeding six, eight or more children, on an agricultural wage, forged inter-dependence, strength of character, a sense of community and fear of being unable to pay the rent. But Norfolk men and women are tenacious and staunch. Field Marshal Montgomery maintained that to take a position he would look to the Scots or the Welsh, but to hold a position he would look to the East Anglians.

North Norfolk has changed a good deal over the last 60 years. Reliance on horses gave way to machinery just before the Second World War. In the post - war years the labour required on the farms was drastically reduced. Where a farm in the 1930s could field one or more cricket teams, this all changed. Cottages lay empty and decaying and there were no longer throngs of children in the streets. Then when the railway closed and the lifeline to the outside world was cut, before the motor car came into more general use, it closed a chapter in the lives of the true villagers. Many of them had travelled to school by train to Wells and Fakenham from the age of 11 from the surrounding district and goods were moved to and from communities by train. Many villages and much of the property fell into a sorry state.

Then in the 1970s Norfolk was discovered as a jewel for holidays and second homes. Property was bought up by Londoners and other 'furriners' at prices well beyond the means of local people. But new industries flourished. Builders, plumbers and decorators became ever more in demand. A new generation of shops opened to satisfy the needs of busy second homers who use their leisure time to buy sophisticated clothes and home furnishings locally. Shopping at the weekend, when there is more time available than in the working week, has encouraged some fashionable boutiques to flourish, notably in Blakeney, Holt and Burnham Market. An abundance of good eating places has followed and North Norfolk is as well served for eating out as any rural area in the country.

Whilst the true villagers may regret the passing of the old days, few want to return to fetching water in a bucket from the pump, emptying it and the contents of the outside loo into a hole in the garden and the hard grind of manual labour that was the daily norm. However, adjustment to new realities is not made easier by the enormous increase in traffic and pressure on amenities, especially in the summer. While the local community has to adjust to the second home and holiday industry the visitors/incomers are happiest when they too adjust to the countryside with its smells and noises and different pace and charm.

It is best not to be in too much of a hurry in Norfolk and, if tempted to queue barge, be aware that the informally dressed 'local' in the queue in front may well be a High Court judge or Fellow of the Royal Society. Appearances are deceptive in the countryside. As one articulate true villager put it, 'Some visitors seem to think we are yokels with hay sticking out of one ear and straw out of the other.' The true villagers who have worked hard all their lives, raised their families, probably fought for their country, are just as interesting as the visitors who doubtless also have their stories to tell. In short, North Norfolk has a rich mixture of characters, whether they have lived here all their lives, or moved in with their wealth and talent because they have come to appreciate this very special part of England.

As to the memories themselves, these can fade after 50 years or so and take on an element of myth or be vested with enchantment or embellishment. Whilst striving for accuracy, I hope my readers will accept that the human memory is fallible. It is all the more interesting for that. Writers who try to achieve infallibility either never start, or are less likely to finish, writing a book. They suffer from the same condition as the dart player who cannot let go of the dart. There is a sense of urgency about recording the memories of elderly people. I want them to have some years to enjoy seeing themselves in print while readers find pleasure in sharing those experiences.

Telling the tale is one thing but seeing one's own words in print for the first time, is another. I am grateful to the contributors to this book for their help as we worked together on the finished chapters.

Raymond Monbiot

Eastgate House
Burnham Market

About the Author

Raymond Monbiot was born in 1937, went to school in London and started work as a trainee with J. Lyons & Co. in 1956 humping sacks of flour for the bakery. Trained as a pastry chef, where his duties included making the cakes for Buckingham Palace garden parties, he moved into production management, including foreman on the nightshift, became a van salesman and rose in the ranks to be the National Sales Manager of Lyons Bakery at the age of 24. He managed companies for Lyons until becoming Managing Director of Huntley & Palmers, Jacobs and Peek Frean biscuits and later Chief Executive of Campbells Soups at King's Lynn. He is a Liveryman of the Worshipful Company of Butchers, a Freeman of the City of London and, for his political and public services, was awarded the MBE in 1981 and the CBE in 1994. He is a columnist and contributor to trade magazines. His first book – *How to Manage Your Boss* – sold 30,000 copies and his first book about North Norfolk – *The Burnhams Book of Characters and Memories* – has been very successful.

In 1961 he married Rosalie Gresham Cooke whose father was a Member of Parliament and whose family has owned the Friary at Blakeney since 1911 – managed today by her brother, the Revd Hereward Cooke, canon of Norwich Cathedral and a Norwich City Councillor. Rosalie is Norfolk County Councillor for the Hunstanton Ward, Chairman of the County Council's Social Services Committee and Chairman of the Board of Visitors of Wayland Prison. She is also Chairman of a national housing association. She was awarded the OBE in 1992.

They live in Burnham Market and have two surviving children. George Monbiot is a well known environment activist, journalist, columnist and author. Eleanor, who lives in Kenya, has extensive responsibilities at World Vision, the second largest humanitarian aid organisation in the world.

Rosalie Monbiot OBE

The Burnhams
Burnham Overy

Leslie and Betty Harvey

Leslie Harvey was born at the family home in Gents Yard, Burnham Market, in 1918. His father, William, was from Burnham Norton and worked on the land as well as renting a 12–acre smallholding. His grandfather, Robert Harvey, came from the North.

Leslie Harvey tells his story. "I went to school in Burnham Market where there were eight classes. The top class was known as Ex7 and I reached it at the early age of 13. I hated history, was no good at music, but could do mental arithmetic as fast as any machine in those days. I could have gone on to Grammar School having passed my 11+ but my father needed me. My mother was ill and died when I was 15 and my brother had a congenital heart disease. He always looked unwell as a boy and the teachers would tell the other boys not to rough him around. He was to undergo replacement of a heart valve at the age of 45, the oldest man to date to have the operation. He lived for another eight years and died at 53.

"My father worked all hours as a land worker and, with his own rented smallholding and family illness, he needed my help. I had fed the chickens at a very early age, perhaps six or seven years old and, on Saturday mornings sometimes, I would feed the sheep. On return from school, I would help with the pigs and chickens.

"My father was a kind and gentle man who would ask rather than command me to do things to help him. He would show me the right way to do things, at each season of the year, such as at lambing time and harvest time. On leaving school I did a paper round for William Lane, newsagent of Front Street. He sold sweets and was also the undertaker. He used to whistle in a persistent soft, blowing sort of way which irritated his customers and caused us children-and others-to laugh.

"I worked with my father who earned about 30 shillings a week. He gave me part of his wages in exchange for my help with his pigs and smallholding. We grew barley, sugar beet and turnips and mangles for the sheep. According to the season, he would cycle to work at Muckleton, to thresh corn by feeding the threshing machine. It was a day's work to make a stack. We paid rent for our cottage of 2 shillings a week to John Gent, who did local repair work to property.

"I always had too much to do, helping my father, to get involved with the local gang and their pranks. We all had nicknames in those days. My brother was nicknamed Moses and I was Aaron. I did however find time for sport. At school I ran relay races versus Fakenham and others, on Cook's Meadow, and won four or five silver medals. We had a regular team, members which included Bob Roy (Philip's son) and Arthur Crow. I was also keen on football and rounders and, when I was a teenager, I trained by running some evenings up Silver Pits Hill which was exactly a mile each way.

" I took up boxing and entered a tournament in Fakenham, when I was 19, as a light middle weight. I remember I had a boil on my leg at the time and covered up the bandage with my sock, so the medical officer would not see it and disqualify me from competing. I won the competition and a silver cup, but gave up the sport soon after. At light middle weight, opponents came in all shapes and sizes. Some of them were 6 feet tall and had a far longer reach with which I could not compete.

"Electricity was only just coming to Burnham Market. Those who converted to it received a free plug and three light bulbs. Most households and farms used heating oil or paraffin and I took a job with Anglo American Oil who had a distribution depot in Burnham Market. I was mate to Billy Moore, the Commer truck driver, and we delivered paraffin and cans of heating oil to farms, shops and garages. I stayed with Billy when others were leaving to find other work and in recognition of my loyalty, he gave me his commission and taught me how to drive.

"Because I was under age, I learned on estate roads rather than the highway and by the age of 17 I was an accomplished driver. However, times were changing and, at the age of 18, I was laid off. I went to drive and work for the stonemason Arthur Potter. I delivered and erected headstones in churchyards and passed my driving test whilst I was with him. He was a wonderful tradesman.

"When war broke out I was 20 years old. Under a scheme introduced for peacetime by Government Minister, Leslie Hore Belisha, young men were given the choice of six months military training, and three and a half years on the reserve list, or transfer to the coal mines. However the outbreak of war changed all this and I was called up 12 days after war was declared on 15th September 1939. I joined the Royal Norfolk Regiment, to which Norfolkmen and others were being drafted from as far away as India and the North West Frontier. I spent 18 months at Britannia barracks in Norwich as a driving instructor and driver on ordinary civilian vehicles. This included three months on a vehicle fitters course.

"After church parade on Sunday we had a few hours off and eight of us would travel by car dropping off at Fakenham, Rudham and then on to Burnham Market. On return to Norwich one evening we saw two army cooks stranded near Guist. They piled into the car – four across the front seats and five in the rear. This distorted the car's braking system and we nearly came to grief at the crossroads at the bottom of a steep hill entering Norwich. Cars were crossing in front of us and I needed all my driving instructor skills to avoid a terrible accident.

"One hundred of us were deputed to attend church on Sunday mornings to represent the army in Norwich. The turnout was usually 99 with one absentee, for whom we covered at roll call, as he went to get the car ready for our quick getaway after the service. We only had petrol for 50 miles which would have taken us to Fakenham and back, so we kept the engine running and put in some paraffin to do the extra miles."

The course of true love brought Leslie to Burnham Overy, where he had met Betty. On one day he cycled on his father's bike three journeys from Cromer to Overy and back. That was 75 miles in all. As Betty recalls, "We had met on the bank at Overy Staithe and I asked Leslie to sign my

autograph book. We girls all had them in those days and used to compete for the most signatures. I was born in Overy and we lived in a house in

Red Row. My father was in the Royal Navy and my grandfather, Joseph Wilby – my mother's father – was a skilled landsman and champion thatcher. He won many a thatching competition, including first prize for the Fakenham area. He was a good and gentle man who walked to work each day to Marsh House Farm from Overy. There were 60 children in Overy in those days and the street was always full of them, playing and making their own amusements.

"Leslie and I saw each other whenever we could, but it was not easy in wartime. Nevertheless we were married in August 1943 – 59 years ago."

After 18 months at Norwich, Leslie was posted for a year to Attleborough as a vehicle mechanic and driver for officers on occasions. Then his posting took him to Gifford House on Putney Common, London. After a short while he was surplus to requirements and drafted for service in Madagascar.

"On a Friday I was told to report to Hull docks for embarkation on the following Monday. However circumstances had caused me to have no leave for seven months and an overseas posting, known as a 'python' scheme, meant no leave for two or three years. So I asked if I could go home for the weekend to see my father. This was granted, providing I promised to be back in Putney on the Monday in time to move out to Hull.

" The officer who gave me permission did not believe I could do it but I gave him my word. I had about four hours at home before starting back and, as I entered the parade ground at Gifford House I heard my name being called. I was on draft and had to be passed medically fit. They asked to look in my mouth and found that I had some teeth missing, but no plate. This was not acceptable because I would not be able to eat special rations and they withdrew me from the draft to Hull.

"I was moved to the Y list, which was a holding category for those who waited to become fit and ready for active service. I was attached to a category battalion at Coltishall. This was made up of A2 to C3 fitness category men which meant that they were not 100% fit. The CO, Colonel Floyd, lived at Brancaster and I became his occasional driver and fitter. It suited him well to have me in the battalion and, whilst the only thing wrong with me was the loss of some teeth, I stayed in the battalion for 15 months.

"On one occasion, Brigadier Templer came to inspect us, a part of his assessment of the state of readiness of East Anglia as a potential invasion zone. It was a very wet day and his car was giving a great deal of trouble starting. His driver was obviously in need of help so I offered it. I knew it was water in the pipes and it had to be drained and dried out. I was emerging from under the car when the Brigadier returned from his inspection. 'What is that man doing under my car?' he demanded of his driver. It was explained that I had been helping get it started. So he looked me up and down, asked me what category I was, and I told him it was A1. 'Then what are you doing in a category battalion?' The CO said I was the man he wanted and the Brigadier let it pass. So I stayed on with Colonel Floyd and we were posted to Dod's holiday camp at Caister which had been requisitioned by the War Office.

Colonel Floyd offered to take his battalion to Italy on garrison duties and said he was seeking permission to do so. He wanted me to be his motor transport sergeant. In view of the likelihood of a 'python' posting the battalion was divided into two, to take pre embarkation leave. I chose to be in the later half because Betty and I had arranged to be married in June 1943 and the dates would fit.

" The Colonel's request to take us to Italy was allowed. My leave was cancelled and I was to be drafted to Scotland for amphibious training, prior to D Day landings. The Colonel tapped the calendar with his cane, and decided he could grant me five days leave. My kit had all to be checked and I was to report back to Caister. He wanted me to bring his car back to Brancaster, but when he found it had broken down and was in Delves garage in Norwich, I was granted a further day's leave to sort it out. As it happened, Betty was in Scotland as a ladies' maid to the family she worked for and we bought an engagement ring in Fraserburgh. I was stationed first at Dumfries and then, ever further north, until I reached Forres.

"I was given five days leave and Betty and I were married in Overy Church in August 1943. As D Day approached we were posted to Southampton to await embarkation. All outgoing mail was prohibited for three weeks before D Day and, although we had no confirmation of where or when we were going, when we were issued with French francs it was a good guess, by no means a certainty, knowing the record of the army, that we were headed for France! The battalion landed at H+2. That is two hours after the first troops went ashore. However, because the 'mulberry' landing harbour broke in two, it was five days before we could land the heavy trucks and tanks.

" Eventually we embarked on a landing ship and, once in position, we drove off the ramp into the water. We had no idea where the Norfolks were and the MP directing the traffic had no idea either. He said just keep going because I was blocking the vehicles behind. After a mile I found we were in the front line, facing a sign that said 'dust means death'. The troops were dug in and not moving, to avoid giving their positions away in the face of heavy and continuous shellfire.

"I was told to reverse and get out at once, as we were presenting a target that would endanger everyone. So I turned round, headed back and made contact at last with the man with the code breaking book which told him where we should be heading. We stayed in the area for five weeks, living on special rations, with no bread until breakout day on 19th July. D Day had been on 6th June. The order was to capture Caen before dark but the Germans threw everything at our battalion and we had to take refuge in a wood, where we made a stand and held them off. Eventually we were able to move forward and cross the River Orne and so on through France to Holland and Bremen in Germany. It took 11 months.

" After peace was declared we spent some time in the former steel town of Solingen in Germany. I was two or three months waiting to be demobilised in Northampton in 1946. I came home to Burnham Overy Staithe where Betty and I lived in Rose Cottage in Wells Road.

Rose Cottage, Overy Staithe

"For a while I worked in the scrap trade and recovered old steel parts, traction engines and other metals. I also bought and sold rabbit skins and pheasant tail feathers. I moved around, working on farms for contractors and then in 1956 I decided I needed some lighter work. I became chauffeur to Mrs Carruthers of Burnham Overy and Betty and I moved into her Lodge Cottage. I used to drive her to Norwich and to London, where she spent some time. Then I would return and look after the house and the dogs." Betty adds, "Part of Mrs Carruthers' house made me nervous. There seemed to be some sort of presence in one of the rooms and I would always run past it. There were tales of smugglers in years gone by and maybe it was something to do with them. I used to cook dinners at the house from time to time." "She is an excellent cook," adds Leslie, keen to pay her a tribute, and he ought to know after 59 years of marriage to Betty.

She continues, " The local shop was owned by Jimmy Riches and we used to stand at the top of Red Row and watch for Bernard Phillips' grandfather. He wore plus-fours and we referred to him as Daddy Phillips. If we were at the shop when he came in he would buy us sweets, so we made sure we were there. My grandmother brought up George Cleaver who was a well known

Overy Staithe

character in Overy. I used to call him uncle but I am not sure that he really was related in that way.

"These were wonderful days for us children. We would look up at the sky and see it was going to be fine, so we took our food, wrapped in newspaper and walked to the beach along the bank. I used to deliver the telegrams for Riches, and he would give me sweets for doing so. One day I had to run all the way down to the beach with a telegram and he gave me half a crown.

"The guests at the Moorings Hotel used to sit outside on the lawn and they would throw coins to the boys swimming in the Haven End, who would dive for them. In those days there was trade in winkles found under the big stones and rocks along the Bank. We used to gather sea lavender and earn a few coppers.

"Later I worked in the Ship House for Mrs Matthew Smith. She lost two sons in the war. I was in her kitchen, making an egg custard, when the telegram arrived giving her the terrible news of the death of one of them. She was the bravest woman I know and put her arm around me. Her second son was killed a short while later but she bore up so well. I also cooked Sunday lunch for Mrs Russell Smith, Audrey Earle's mother. We cooked a huge joint for the family and a whole cod for the cats."

Leslie was with Mrs Carruthers for six years before going to the Bircham Construction College where he stayed for 16 years. He then looked after the gardens of a number of houses in Burnham Market. He is still working a few hours and continues with his British Legion poppy selling house to house.

Betty was warden at Sutton Lea for many years. "I had to be available 24 hours a day but I found the job very rewarding and I really enjoyed it. I think I gave it up too soon. If one of the residents needed help they rang a bell, which sounded in my house and switched on a red light outside their own. I would come out of the house and look for the light to know which one it was. One night when it was very dark I saw a white shape in front of me and thought it was the person who needed help, coming out to find me. But it turned out to be a flower bed."

Betty and Leslie have three children. Stephanie works in the chemist shop in Burnham Market, Marie lives in Weymouth where she is in charge of 70 carers and Daniel works at Sandringham. They have five grandchildren and two great grandchildren.

June Dye

June Raven was the youngest of nine children, born in 1947 to John and Lilly Raven of Gong Lane, Burnham Overy Staithe.

"We were a very close family even though 18 years separated the eldest and me. I had five sisters and three brothers and we had an idyllic childhood in Overy Staithe. We spent most of our time out of doors, playing and making our own amusements. Every Sunday, summer and winter, we would walk on the beach in all weathers. There were loads of kids in the village in those days. Each autumn we would walk in Holkham Park and collect nuts for our parents. We would scrump apples from the orchards in the village, especially when the fair arrived on the green opposite the end of New Road. We were promised a free ride if we supplied the showmen with some apples. We never got our free ride and fell for it every year.

"Miss Riches, sister of the owner of the village shop, had a plum tree. She would make cones out of newspaper and give them to us to fill with plums to eat. There was a bench outside the pub and we would gather there around the roadmender, Cuckoo Moorhouse, who could imitate any bird and had a fund of stories. He had a brother called Matey. He was a gypsy, with enormously bushy hair, and an arresting personality. We listened to him wide eyed.

There was also Inez Bell who would tell us stories as we congregated around her gate, just across the road from the Hero.

"We collected fuel for our November 5th bonfire, which was built in the field at the top of Gong Lane. My father would bring the horse and cart from the farm and he and my brothers would go around cutting the hedges, making fuel for the bonfire. We kids would go round the houses and collect suitable rubbish. Everyone would save it for us and the bonfire grew to an enormous size. Then on bonfire night, all the kids would gather around it, shouting for my Dad to light it which he did every year. We roasted potatoes in the fire and ran around it in the dark. We never had fireworks but it did not matter.

"Another favourite occasion was St Valentine's Day when we would make and wrap little presents for our friends and leave them on their doorstep. It was a great thrill to receive a Valentine's present and try to guess who sent it.

My mother would search through any pieces she might have hidden away to help us make the little gifts and participate in the excitement. She was a great contributor to the neighbourhood and in the war she was active in the Salvation Army – with many a story to tell.

"There was always someone coming to the door – 'Can you help, Lilly?' She could charm warts away and people were always phoning her or coming to the door for advice to get rid of them. Unfortunately she took the secret with her when she died. I can see her now, in summer, sitting just inside the front door, a cigarette in her mouth, a child on her lap and a newspaper, with neighbours passing by or calling with their troubles.

"My parents could not afford many presents for us at Christmas. We were a large family and the large ones tended to be the poorest, before state support eased the burden. But we would not have known it. We felt we counted in their affections, wanted for nothing and made our own amusements. At Christmas we would sit in a row with our backs turned to Mother and try to guess what she had in her hand. I used to peek and cheat a bit. We also played 'spin for the apple'. The apple would be cut up into pieces and placed like the hours of a clock. Then each of us would spin a knife in turn and, wherever it pointed on coming to rest, entitled the spinner to the nearest piece of apple. In winter the dyke on the other side of the bank would freeze and we slid about on it. When it snowed we sledged down Gong Lane.

"We loved harvest time. We would ride on the horses and join my Dad and the other grown ups for their lunch sitting in the hedgerows. When the corn was threshed, we tried to catch the mice that were driven out of it. Such innocent pleasures would not be allowed today, when children are no longer allowed near farm machinery and, in any case, the old methods of harvesting have long since given way to less labour intensive practices.

"We were never alone as children and had a great sense of family. I loved my school days in Overy School, with Miss Ede and Miss Drury, as much as I detested them when I moved to Burnham School at the age of 11 where, if you did not have money, you were ignored by the teachers and treated differently to the others. I felt continually put down and unappreciated. For example, in sewing, while some of the girls were making aprons and such like, I was put to sewing a square. As soon as I brought it to the teacher, finished, she commanded that I unpick it and start again.

"My experience at Burnham School, in those days, ruined my life. It sapped my confidence and has caused me problems on and off for years.

Burnham School is so different today. The staff are a joy to work with and the atmosphere is quite different to the misery of selective exclusion I experienced in my own school days. I suppose that, coming from a poor family, our clothes stood out from those who could afford better. It did not matter at Overy School but it did at Burnham – then.

"My father, John, worked on Satchells' Farm in Overy Staithe. It is no longer there having been turned into housing. My mother worked at the Moorings Hotel during its happy days. When I left school at 15 in 1962, I too went to work at the Moorings. I started there washing up and then promoted myself to chambermaid. Some lovely people stayed there, many famous names among them. Our favourite was a Lord who came for just one night and left a tip of £5. This was a lot of money in those days. We pooled all the tips and divided them out. The Moorings used to shut in October each year and I then went to work on the land sorting carrots and potatoes. When the hotel re-opened in March we would all be back there for the season. Mrs Muriel Phillips and her husband George were a delight to work for.

"In 1968 I married Al Dye. We had known each other for about a year, having first met when Beryl Bickell and I were sitting on the Quay at Wells,

Hero

giving the eye to promising young men. We used to whistle at them to engage their interest. Then we would make off in the car, hoping they would follow. Amongst these young men were Al and a mate of his, who played the game and would join up with us for a drink. Al is the only boyfriend I have ever had. He is a skilled carpenter and now works for Kitchens Etc. in North Creake.

"When we were first married, we searched for a place where we could afford to live. This took us as far as Shouldham, near Downham Market. It was a tiny village and I was very lonely. We lived in a caravan for five years after that and I went to work for Campbells in King's Lynn, for a year, preparing vegetables and chicken for their soups. I felt I was not being promoted as I should and moved on to work for Pye, assembling black boxes for television sets. I stayed there for about three years.

" Al worked for a contractor as a carpenter at the time. Then for a while I worked for an engineering firm, soldering circuit boards, before going back to work at the Moorings. At the time, the Council were building bungalows in Overy and I badgered them every day for one. In 1973 I succeeded.

"When the Moorings changed hands, I left and went to work for four years for Mrs Atkinson, who had a large house at the T junction at the end of New Road. In 1977 I was expecting our son, Wesley. I had lost a baby in 1971, which was a very stressful experience. When Wesley arrived I gave up work for three years until we moved to Burnham Market, to the house in Church Walk where we still live.

"So that I could always be at home when Wesley returned from school, I took a number of part-time jobs, cleaning and caring for second homes and, later, for the Carpenters at Church Close next door. I also worked for many years for Mrs Phyllis Roy who lived in Station Road. I eventually developed a good relationship with her but she was not always easy to get along with. I learned how to cope with her moods. For example, if she said something unwelcoming in the morning, I would pick up my coat and make for the door, even though I had just arrived. She would ask where I thought I was going and I would say that I was not going to work for her if she was in a mood. She would laugh and it was back to normal. I developed a very good relationship with her over the years. She became like a mother to me and depended upon me, during her progressive illness, until she died.

"Wesley suffered from dyslexia and could neither read nor write when he left Burnham School for Wells. But there he blossomed. They understood and helped him with his problem. He has overcome so much and passed his qualifications as a plumber, having attended King's Lynn College and residential courses in Luton and Milton Keynes. We are very proud of him and he is a good and reliable plumber.

" I took a job at Burnham School as a cleaner in 1993 and, when the post of caretaker came up, three or four years later, on the retirement of David Wells, I applied for it and was successful. Before David, the caretaker was Donny Scoles. I love the job. Everyone is so friendly. The teachers are good and I feel involved with the kids and the staff. Of course, occasionally I have to 'square them up' but it is all good fun. I make tea for the teachers when they arrive in the morning and expect them to make a cup for me if they make tea in the evening!

Burnham School

"I open up the school each morning after 7 a.m and stay until about 9 a.m, depending how much talking I do, and then return at 3 p.m to clean and lock up at around 6 p.m. The school has a marvellous atmosphere and is getting good reports. The children are all treated equally. I like to help on Sports Day and for the annual fete. The one bright spot in my own school days at Burnham was Annie Franklin's cooking. Her trifle was the best I have ever tasted.

"It is sad that the activities in the village no longer involve people as once they did. The Flower Show used to be the centrepiece of activity in the summer but it has declined over the years. Young people seem reluctant to get involved. I would like to see more activity for the children and, instead of 50p prizes, they should get a medal to keep and show to their friends. There are still some village highlights, however. Burnham Market at Christmas is still magic and people come from miles around to see the lights and the 'switching on', which still captures the atmosphere of the old days.

"I am interested in helping kids with their arts and crafts and we have had great fun making a giraffe out of wire netting and plaster of Paris. I spent some time teaching kids how to knit, but there is a dying interest in this pastime. Another interest which I pursued for many years was my work for the RSPCA.

" One of the events I dreaded most in my life was the eventual death of my mother. She had been the lynchpin of the family for so many years. She continued to live in Overy Staithe until 1981 when she moved into Burnham Market. Her friends had mostly died and she was miserable and unwell and I suppose her death can be counted as a happy release. It was less of a strain for me to have her close until she died in 1989. My surviving brothers and sisters are scattered these days. My eldest sister, Doreen, lives in Bedford but her family comes to visit, particularly at Christmas. Another sister, Tilly Willsher, lives in Overy Town and I also have a sister at Hingham. My brother Eric lives in Overy Town and farms with Hancocks and Maurice is farming in Swaffham. Michael worked for many years in Holkham Hall.

"Al and I have two dogs, Sally and Harry, and we all go off together for holidays in our caravan. I am responsible for the garden which seems to grow bigger every year. I have never been abroad and have no wish to do so – anyway, who would look after the dogs?"

Burnham Thorpe

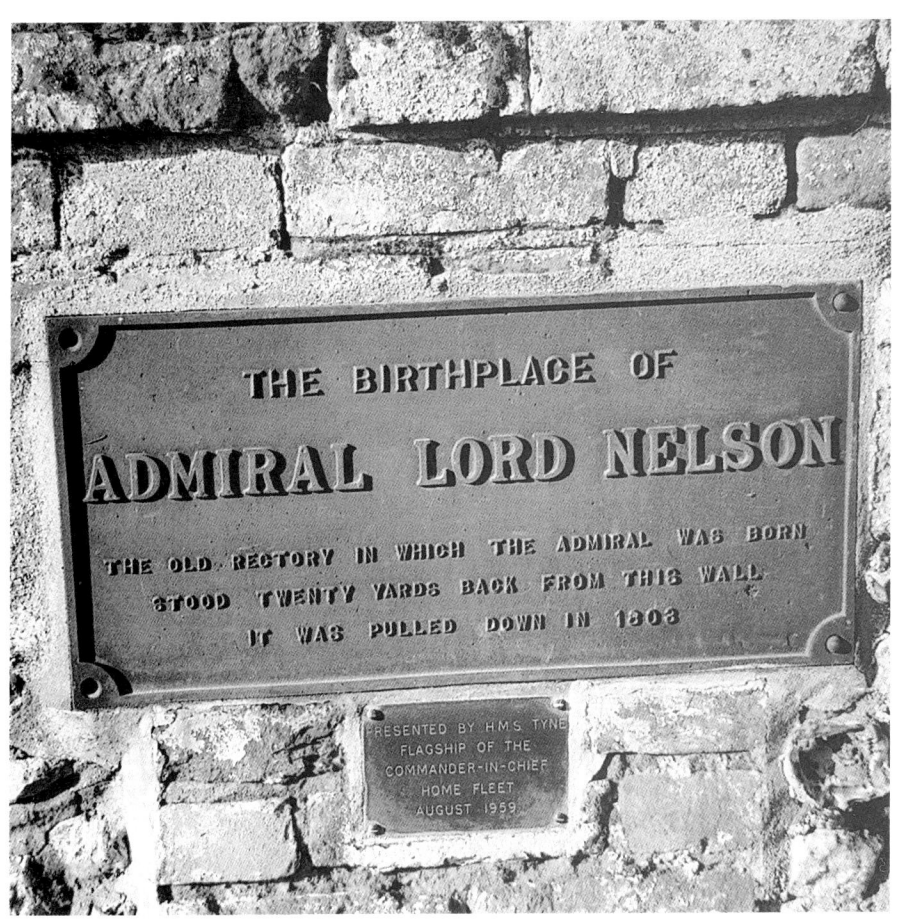

Beryl Alexander

Beryl Neave was born in Burnham Market near the Robins fish shop – later to become Farrows. At the age of four her parents moved with her and her sister Eileen, to Burnham Thorpe and she has lived there ever since. When Beryl was 13, her parents moved within Burnham Thorpe into a three-bedroom house at Number 9, The Pightle, which is the very same house she moved into on her retirement in the year 2000.

"When we moved there all those years ago, from a smaller house, we thought it was a palace. My father was a shepherd but saw a job opportunity as a cowman at Ivy Farm which entitled him to a pint of fresh milk and a can of skimmed milk every day and half a pound of butter every Friday – which he made in the dairy. This was a valuable contribution to the family budget for, with two children and another on the way, money was short. In fact, the family was very hard up and remained so during our childhood, but we children would never have known it. We adored our parents and each other and never had the impression that we were wanting for anything. At Christmas our parents always produced a stocking for us.

"At first my mother hated the move to Burnham Thorpe. There was no tarmac on the roads in those days and she had to walk to Burnham Market to do the shopping on sandy or muddy surfaces according to the weather.

She earned two shillings and six pence for washing the Revd Hibbert's undies on a Monday and seven shillings and sixpence for decorating each room in the rectory, and they were big rooms.

" My two sisters, Eileen and Jo, were outgoing and good at talking to people. I was the shy one and used to go through agonies if I had to perform in public, while they took it all in their stride. They had a lot more to say than I did. Eileen first became a nursery nurse, but when she married, she and her husband took on the licence of the White Hart pub in Hammersmith in London. However, this pub life did not suit them in the long term, so she changed her career and held a good job as a housing officer on Ealing Town Council.

"Eileen died in 1995 which was a great sadness, particularly following the most dreadful year of my life in 1986 when my mother died. Some months later in the same year, my youngest sister, Jo, died of cancer at the age of 57. She was much loved and sorely missed. In her memory, Wells School erected

Beryl and her sisters

a plaque outside her kitchen and dedicated a tree to the service she gave as the cook in charge for many years. The children at Wells also carved a high candlestick in her memory and this is displayed in Thorpe church on every festive occasion. My beloved Dad died in 1989.

"I was taught at Thorpe School by Kate Letzer, mother of Judith Bettison, whose daughter keeps Clothes Line in Burnham Market. We used to go to cookery lessons from school every week, driven by George Hubbard. We had to take food to cook, and in my case, it was usually cheese and potato pie because my parents could not afford anything else. I still make a marvellous cheese and potato pie amongst other good things to eat.

"When I left school I was immediately apprenticed as a hairdresser to the Burnham Market shop in Front Street which is now Fern Cottage. My parents had to find £10 to pay to Lawyer Francis for this apprenticeship, which must have been very difficult for them. I stayed on as a hairdresser for 14 years until the toll on my legs, standing all day, caused the doctor to say that if I did not give it up, it would give me up. I loved the work and, for someone as shy as I was, it was a good way to meet people. My regular customers came every fortnight in those days and I got to know them well.

"I was living above the shop when I married Alec in 1950. We had been going out together for some while. At one stage my attention wandered as I thought the grass might be greener when there were all those soldiers around. However, I realised that Alec and I were meant for each other. He came from East Wretham and his father was a gamekeeper on the Holkham estate. Alec, whose full name was Cyril John Alexander, was called Alec by everyone. He was a great character and he loved dancing, both old time and modern. There was a dance once a month and we used to go to Sculthorpe for lessons. I was 25 when we married and he was 27. Together we lived a very happy life for 43 years until he died in 1993, which broke my heart.

"In 1949 we were offered the hairdressing business in Burnham Market for £500. We did not have the money to buy it and our lives would probably have been very different had we done so. As it was, our daughter Louise was born in 1953 and we moved to 11 Goodricks in Burnham Thorpe. There was so much more going on in the villages at that time. There were many more young people around. The young men worked on the farms and would congregate and chat on the bridge outside the village shop in Thorpe.

" There were two cricket teams – a first and second XI. The cricket field, in the village, was grazed by cows for most of the time, and Alec would never allow a cowpat to get in the way of a dive for the ball. It can be imagined what state he came home in after a game. He was a brilliant

Alec in action

cricketer, and was presented by Bill Edrich with the EDP trophy in 1957 for the best performance in the Sandringham League. His highest score was 102 runs not out, and he was also a demon fast bowler. I have pages of press clippings recording his success as a bowler and batsman.

"Many people, from all parts of Norfolk, would remember Alec through his cricketing performances. Even in the latter days of his life, if he could outperform his opponents, often playing just his wife and daughter and grandchildren, he would show his expertise at the game. Sunday evenings were often spent playing on the meadow at the rear of the Shooting Box but he would always shine, even though he was three times the age of his opponents. He must be the only cricketer to be congratulated for hitting a six through the school room window, to the admiration of the headmistress. One wonders, had there been any money in sport in those days, if that would have been a logical career move for Alec.

"My 43 year association with the Zuckerman family started by chance. At the time they lived in Birmingham and had a holiday home at The Forge in Burnham Thorpe. My mother-in-law – Granny Alec – looked after it for them when they were not there and helped the family when they were. One day she tripped and fell and asked me if I would help until she was recovered. I was asked to stay for a fortnight! Over the next 43 years Solly Zuckerman and his wife Lady Joan, daughter of the Marquis of Reading, were very kind and I was looked upon almost as one of the family.

The Shooting Box, Burnham Thorpe

"When they moved into the Shooting Box, they converted some disused garages into a delightful flat for Alec and me, and a studio for Lady Joan. I became their housekeeper and caretaker and Alec drove Lord Zuckerman, although his main job was working for David and then Teddy Maufe at Branthill Farm, which he did for 51 years. He drove the first combine harvester on the farm. It had no cab and he used to come home looking as if he'd been mining coal. It took bottles of Optrex to get the grit out of his eyes. Such conditions would never be allowed today and many of the cabs on modern agricultural machinery are better than the cars we drive.

"Lady Zuckerman lived permanently at the Shooting Box and Lord Zuckerman would come home on a Friday and leave for work again on a Monday morning. I have known their son Paul since he was 12 and his sister Stella since she was ten. She died tragically in her early forties. Her children Hester and Sebastian are good friends of mine.

The house was frequently full of interesting and distinguished guests. Many famous people dined and stayed there over the years. The highlights were when the Royal visitors came and Alec and I entertained their security staff in our home. House parties were usually for six people plus family and the atmosphere was relaxed and friendly. The Zuckermans had originally got to know the area from their holidays at the Moorings Hotel in Burnham Overy Staithe. They subsequently looked for a house in the area and found The Forge.

"I had an arrangement with Lady Zuckerman in the early days, that I would help her in any way in the house, except waiting at table. I shuddered at the thought of handing round the dishes to her guests and family. Maybe it was something to do with my shyness but I overcame it eventually and waiting at table from time to time had less fears for me as the years went on.

"There were many highlights during all those years with the Zuckerman family. Every January the Queen Mother came to visit. I also remember Lord Jenkins staying in Burnham Thorpe, in hiding to avoid threats from the IRA. Alec had to pick him up from King's Lynn station when he was Home Secretary and was told by the police to drive without stopping, direct to the Shooting Box. He was not to stop for anyone. Alec loved fast cars and being told to drive at high speed. It was a great exhilaration for him. The house on those occasions was surrounded by armed guards.

"Other distinguished guests included the Queen, Sir William Walton, Douglas Fairbanks Jnr, the American Ambassador, Admiral Richover, the

American Chief of Staff, Lord and Lady Chalfont, Prince Charles, Lord Mountbatten, Patricia Mountbatten and Elizabeth Frink the sculptress.

"Lord Zuckerman died in 1993, in the same week as Alec, and this brought Lady Joan and me even closer together. He and Alec had got on well and he liked nothing better than walking round the estate with him. Lady Joan took up painting more seriously after her husband's death and entertained her artistic friends. She gave me a number of her paintings which hang in my home today. I was with her when she died in March 2000 and Lord Peyton spoke at her funeral. It was a very moving occasion. Her last words to me, before she died, were to ask me to look after her little dog. She said she was quite sure I would take good care of the little fellow. Elwyn is with me now, as are Cindy and Jackie, my sister Eileen's dogs.

" I had never owned a dog but now I have three. They are a very important part of my life and reinforce my wish to stay at home. I have never been abroad and have no wish to do so, even though my family is well travelled in their various successful careers.

"Louise, a hearing audiologist, has three children. Billy is a business analyst graduate of The Royal Holloway College, lives in Australia and is doing very well. He phones me every week and sometimes twice a week. Despite the fact that he lives so far away I feel I know him as well as any of my grandchildren. He came to live with me in his holidays from The Royal Holloway College, after Alec died, which was wonderful for me and it helped me a lot. He has promised to come home for my 80th birthday in a few years time. Hannah is a product manager, having taken a degree at the University of East Anglia. Sean, who has done a lot of work with the handicapped, is clever with his hands and is a qualified welder.

"I like to go to church and am a convert from Methodism. As children, we had to go to church three times on a Sunday and I can remember the terrible fears I suffered when I had to prepare to give a recitation on Whit Sunday. My sisters were able to do it without much preparation, but for me it was an awful experience. I told my parents that I could not put up with this and gloomy preachers any longer and no way would I ever put a child of mine through such an ordeal. So I moved to Thorpe Church. I look after six graves at the church – my family and Stella and her mother Lady Joan.

"One of the incidents that sticks in my memory, and of which I am not very proud, was the occasion when I went to surprise my father who was milking a cow. I was eight years old and the cow had a calf. My father was sitting on a milking stool and I crept up and shouted 'boo'. The cow thought this was directed at her and charged me, knocking the stool, the pail and my father flying. I can still see the milk flying to this day. Had it not been for the hurdle in front of the cow it could have been more serious. I fled and told my mother what had happened. Eventually my father came home and said he did not need to tell me off because I already knew what I had done.

"Burnham Thorpe has changed greatly over the last 30 or so years. It used to be inhabited by people who were born within 10 miles, but many of these have been displaced by people from London and the South East, many of whom have second homes here. Nonetheless, many of these newcomers have given a new lease of life to a sleepy village, although there are a few who try to change village life. They seem to think that because they have

The Nelson Hall

moved to the country, country life should be quiet to suit their weekend lifestyle. For example, there used to be many social events at the Nelson Hall, but newcomers to the village have spoiled the opportunities to continue these, complaining of late night noise.

"The Nelson Hall was where we celebrated. It was where Alec and I held our wedding reception, my parents' silver, golden and diamond wedding parties, my sister Jo and Peter her husband's wedding and silver wedding. Alec and I celebrated our ruby wedding there. The hall has always been special to me, reminding us all of such happy times.

"Employment, half a century ago, was mainly working on the farms. But nowadays any younger people have to go to the towns for employment, because the farms are now fully mechanised and only employ one or two people. The holiday homes provide work for part-timers as gardeners and cleaners and there are also opportunities for builders and decorators.

"One of the main employers of the village years ago was John Howard, who for a period of time had a factory pre-packing carrots. Mr Algar and Mr Curry had a carpenters shop, not far from the village shop, and there was a forge where horses were shod. When I was young, the main entertainment was the Cosy Cinema in Burnham Market. There was also a thriving Guide movement to which I belonged when I was 18 years old. This was held in the Lodge owned by Mrs Laboucher. We had no television, and made our own entertainment. The men had a club in the Nelson Hall, playing billiards twice a week, and table tennis. Mrs Mahon used to organise concert parties and Alec used to sing at them.

"In those days there were many more young people and we did not travel by car to the towns. In fact, there were only five cars in the village, owned by the headmistress and the local farmers."

Beryl Alexander has a serenity about her which comes from a warm nature and a happy life. She is a genuinely happy person with a great love of family, dating from her own happy childhood. She has found fulfilment in her own family and in the Zuckerman family which she served so successfully for more than four decades.

Burnham Market

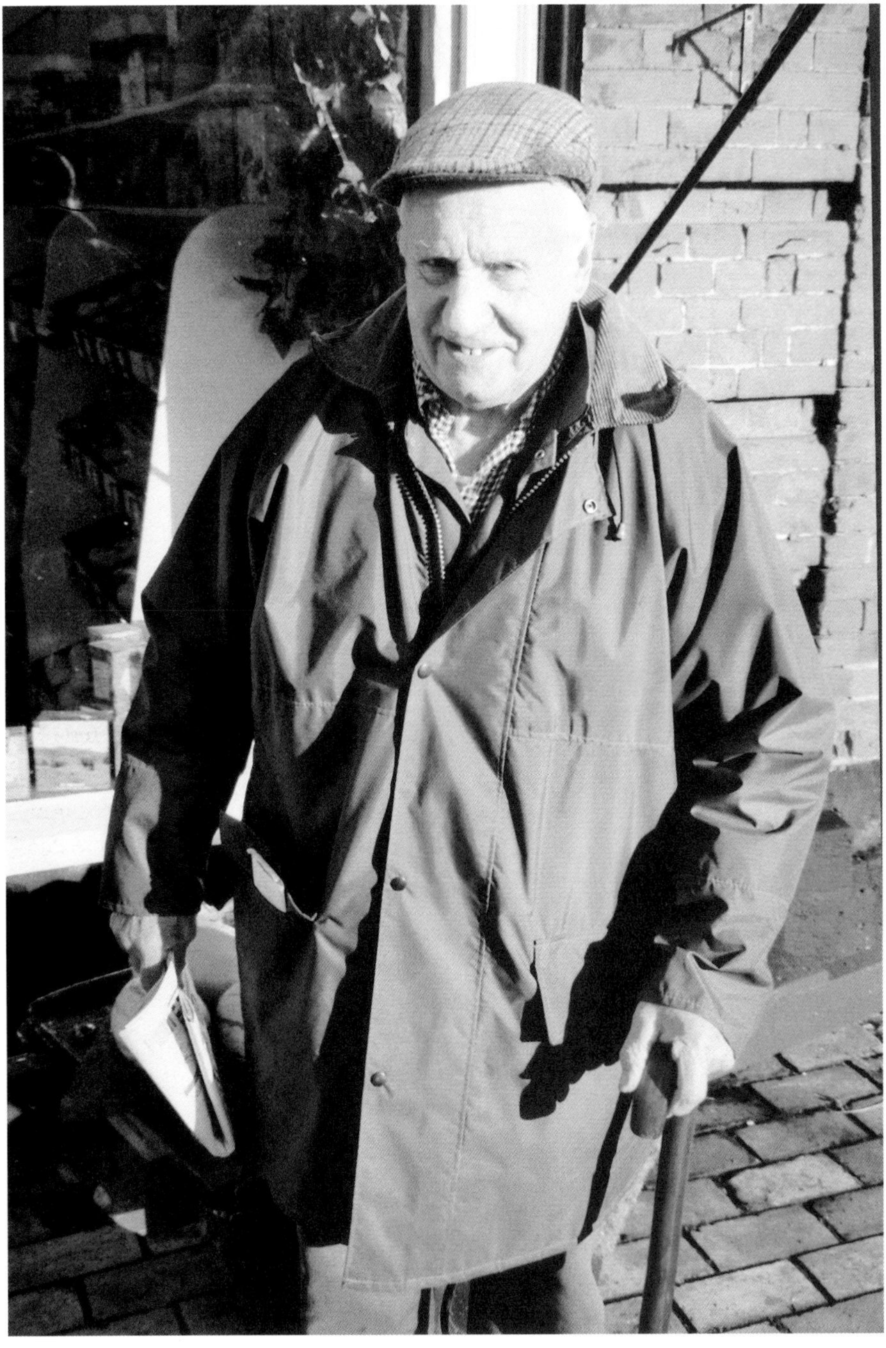

Reg Mussett

In 1903, Reg Mussett's grandfather, who was a Howard, came to live at East End Farm, Burnham Thorpe, then part of the Orford Estate, with connections with Lord Walpole, who is still Lord of the Manor of Burnham Thorpe. The Howards had started on a small farm at Thursford, and progressed to a larger farm at Massingham and then to Cranmer Home Farm before settling at Burnham Thorpe. He was a farmer and coal merchant and had two daughters, one of whom became Mary Heather's mother, and the second, at whose birth his wife died, was Alice Elizabeth who was to become Reg Mussett's mother.

It was impossible for a farmer to bring up two daughters on his own and he had to engage a housekeeper. In due course he married the housekeeper and they had two more children. Thus the Howard household had four children who were brought up together.

Reg picks up the story: "My father, Alfred Oscar Mussett, served throughout the First World War and came through without a scratch. He then went into pig and poultry farming at Dersingham on a rented paddock. One of the characters of Dersingham in those days was Emma Thornton who did the rounds, with her horse and cart, selling paraffin and household goods. She used to have a donkey, but it died. Few people had ever seen a dead donkey, so she would bring it in the cart and ask for contributions towards the spectacle. She collected enough to buy a horse.

"We moved to 136-acre Gallow Hill Farm on the Stanhoe Road at the western end of Burnham Market, which we rented off the Holkham Estate, in 1929. Then in 1944, the first Earl of Leicester, having died in his 90s, to be followed shortly after by the death of the second Earl, who died after falling down the cellar steps, the Estate was faced with heavy death duties. They had to sell off some farms and my father bought Gallow Hill Farm. The Mussetts have farmed it ever since and, having bought an additional field, it now extends to 146 acres, growing mainly malting barley and sugar beet, and grazing up to 20 cattle."

In 1975 Reg Mussett married the redoubtable Mary Trett, daughter of George Trett the baker. Mary's mother, Olive, was a Hudson, a distinguished Burnham family for many generations. Her grandfather, George Hudson,

Gallow Hill

was Clerk to the Parish Council and a saddler and harness maker. He was also on the Board of Overy School and Burnham School and lived at Holly House, now renamed Vine House, next to Grooms. There were two holly trees in the garden from which he made whips. His son George, who was an uncle to Mary Mussett, sold the Westgate Hall Estate land to Mr Sherar in 1934 and the Hall itself to another buyer, reputedly for £5000.

Mary Mussett continues. "My mother married George Trett, whose father, William Trett, was a confectioner and had a mineral water factory in Great Yarmouth. This is now the Lacon Brewery. When my father's mother died he married again."

Reg Mussett went to Burnham School. Born in 1923, he was of that same, good vintage of Burnham characters as John Utting, Stanley Baldwin and Harry Farrow. They were taught by Mr Newell who was also the Scout Master and who lived opposite the Day Centre. Other teachers were Mr Keeble, the strict headmaster who frequently used the cane, and Miss Burge. Then Reg went on to Wells School and later attended machinery education evening classes at Burnham Thorpe as the era of the horse gave way to mechanisation.

"We had to pass exams on what we had been taught," he says. "We had our first tractor on the farm in 1939. The only vet in the village years ago had to be fetched if there was a need for his services because he had no car.

However, he liked his drink, and on one occasion, when my father collected him, he could not make out whether he was treating a horse or a cow. My father decided he would take him home again. We used the Rudham vets for years and they were very good."

Mary and Reg can both remember Oily Smith delivering paraffin and other hardware and Billy Moore who worked for Pratts, the forerunner of Esso, who brought petrol to the farms by lorry. Percy Taylor was another roundsman who carried household goods and farm sundries in a horsedrawn cart from Creake. Burgess had a fish delivery by horse and cart and so did Willis."

Mary continues, " If we went to Yarmouth we could buy a cran of herring for a shilling and we would bring them back in an old sack and pass them out to friends. The poorest families would eat what was available to them and most would have old hare soup on the go - a pennyworth of bones and scraps from the cooking. And bread and milk.

"Miss Disney, a well known character, lived for years in a beach hut at Overy Staithe with three horseshoes over the door and named *The Third Shoe,* following her retirement as a gymnastics teacher at Roedean School. She always wore a gymslip or navy shorts and never wore shoes. She devised a fish pudding, made from cockles, samphire and fish – all readily available, for those who sought them, and it became a welcome local speciality. When the beach huts were removed, Miss Disney lived at the end of Billy Haines' boat house, in a flat that could only be reached by climbing a ladder. My father found three iron cannon balls about the size of bowling woods on Gun Hill.

"Jack Marsh was a notorious character and often in trouble with the law. He was always being blamed for something, rightly or wrongly, and stories of his exploits abound in the village. He was a very strong and energetic man. Most families from the cottages had allotments in a 10 acre field at the northern end of Gallow Hill Farm. Jack Marsh dug a strip the whole length of the 10 acre field to grow food for his family.

"Fred Baldwin used to offer a cat castration service in his spare time, from his job as cowman. He would put the cat in a bag, with a hole in it, so the tail could stick out, then he would get on with the business. One cat, given him for castration, turned out to be a 10 year-old female."

While there was great poverty in those days there was a sense of community. Mary remembers, "The children of the village spent much of their time in and out of each others' houses, which were never locked, and played outdoors making their own amusements. The Goose Bec was a source of endless games. It flowed along the surface of Front Street and we would have jumping poles to help us leap across the flow. Where it disappeared temporarily from view, into a culvert, we would have Pooh-stick competitions and send messages.

"As we had no garden at the bakery in Front Street, I would go and play with my friend Mary Belton who lived at Crabbe Hall Farm. It was a habit for people to sit on the wall by Stilgoe's corner, watching cricket or football, and Mary and I would look around in the leaves for the pennies that fell out of their pockets.

"I went to St Monica's School in Burnham Overy Staithe which, at the time, cost £3 a term. Then, following the traditions of my family, I went on to King's Lynn High School, now renamed Springwood. In those days there was fierce rivalry between Overy and Burnham, and Thorpe and Burnham. Each village tended to lead more separate lives. My father, George, supplied bread to the villages in the district and I became one of his delivery roundsmen.

"We used to graze the horses in Cook's Meadow along the Overy Road. After work each day I would cycle, leading a horse. Sometimes, with no halter, the horse would just follow, being quite clear where it was going. It would stand quietly while I parked the bike near the gate and opened up for the horse to enter the field. However, if I was a bit slow, the horse would show its impatience with a good nudge with its nose from behind. One of my parents' horses, which had been retired to the meadow, broke out, during the war, after a stick of bombs fell nearby, and trotted home to the bakery. We searched for the silver foil, anti radar strips, which we used for Christmas decorations.

"We had a coal oven at the Bakery in Front Street, and at Christmas time we would cook turkeys for those without an oven big enough at home. On one occasion I can remember the Misses Cook having a turkey delivered to be roasted. Jack Langley, the deaf and dumb boy who minded the oven, made grimaces to my mother, when she returned some while later, indicating a bad smell from the oven. We found that the Misses Cook had forgotten to take out the insides of the turkey.

"They were kind and thoughtful people and did a lot for the young of the village. When they got older, they had to fend more for themselves without the staff to care for them, and found it difficult to cope with the practicalities of running a house. However they had some loyal friends including Miss Savory who lived with them and Ann Everitt.

"When the Misses Cook died, the sale of the Eastgate House contents took place in the Nelson Hall at Burnham Thorpe, and people were concerned to see items, such as a stone doll, that they thought belonged to Sutton Church. The truth is that the Misses Cook had lent the church these items, and many more besides, over the decades they worshipped there. We used to play games in their meadow as children. There were goats grazing and we would catch newts in the pond, hanging over it from a projecting branch. Just under the tree is a spring and when the pond was low we would dig down to it and put in a barrel with no bottom, to provide the horses with a drink.

"At the time, the granary barn at Roys' Mill was in a direct line with the top of Cook's Meadow and if we shouted from there, the echo of our voices would come back to us. Regrettably the barn was pulled down years ago."

Reg recalls the eccentric Oliver family who lived in the house where Barclays Bank now stands. They were three bachelor brothers and a sister, all living there together, with their own separate cupboards for food. Alice, Oliver, and Fred, one of her brothers, never appeared. John, another brother, was very religious and a church warden. He had an allotment where he grew the vegetables, which he sold by wheeling them around the village in panniers on a bicycle he never rode. The other brother, Jimmy, was completely different. He bred and broke in ponies for riding and driving.

"During the floods in 1953 he had upwards of 20 horses on the marshes, and everyone who could handle horses went to help him bring them to safety. They all survived and were penned in the pound temporarily. The Olivers were reputed to be a wealthy family whose money came, it was said, from the brewery at Creake."

Mary recalls: "Jimmy Oliver was among the bakery's customers who brought rabbits to be cooked. He would bring two skinned and cleaned rabbits in a pan. He never took the heads off, but the eyes had been removed to make room for herbs. There were many families who ate cold rabbit pie for breakfast on Christmas Day. When cooked, the juices from the rabbit formed a jelly which helped to make a lovely moist pie.

"One of our regular customers at the baker's shop was Major Combe, husband of Lady Sylvia. He was a real gentleman of the old school and would regularly buy a cottage loaf to take to his Board meetings at Watney, Combe and Reid in London. He always carried a lucky five-shilling piece.

If he left it behind at home by mistake it would be sent on to him wherever he was. We thought it might have been a lucky talisman which helped to see him through the First World War. My father died in 1951 and Mother and I carried on the business until she died on exactly the same day, and I think at the same hour, 10 years later in 1961.

"I then became a teacher for 14 years at the Old Hall preparatory school at Hethersett, teaching six to seven year olds, until I married Reg and moved to Gallow Hill Farm in 1975. Reg, who had lived with his mother at the farm until she died in 1974, spent one winter there all on his own. We had known each other for 25 years and sort of drifted into it."

Reg Mussett, who employed two contractor farm hands until one died recently, now works the farm with just one person.

"Farming is so much less labour intensive today. Mary has certainly done her share on the farm. In the very hot summer of 1976, when it was impossible to work during the heat of the day, Mary and I were up at 4 a.m to get it done. Mary drove the tractor. We built the bungalow we now live in. The old farmhouse is still there but empty."

Gallow Hill Farm is the first landmark one sees on entering Burnham Market from the west. It is appropriate that it is in the hands of two of the oldest families in the area.

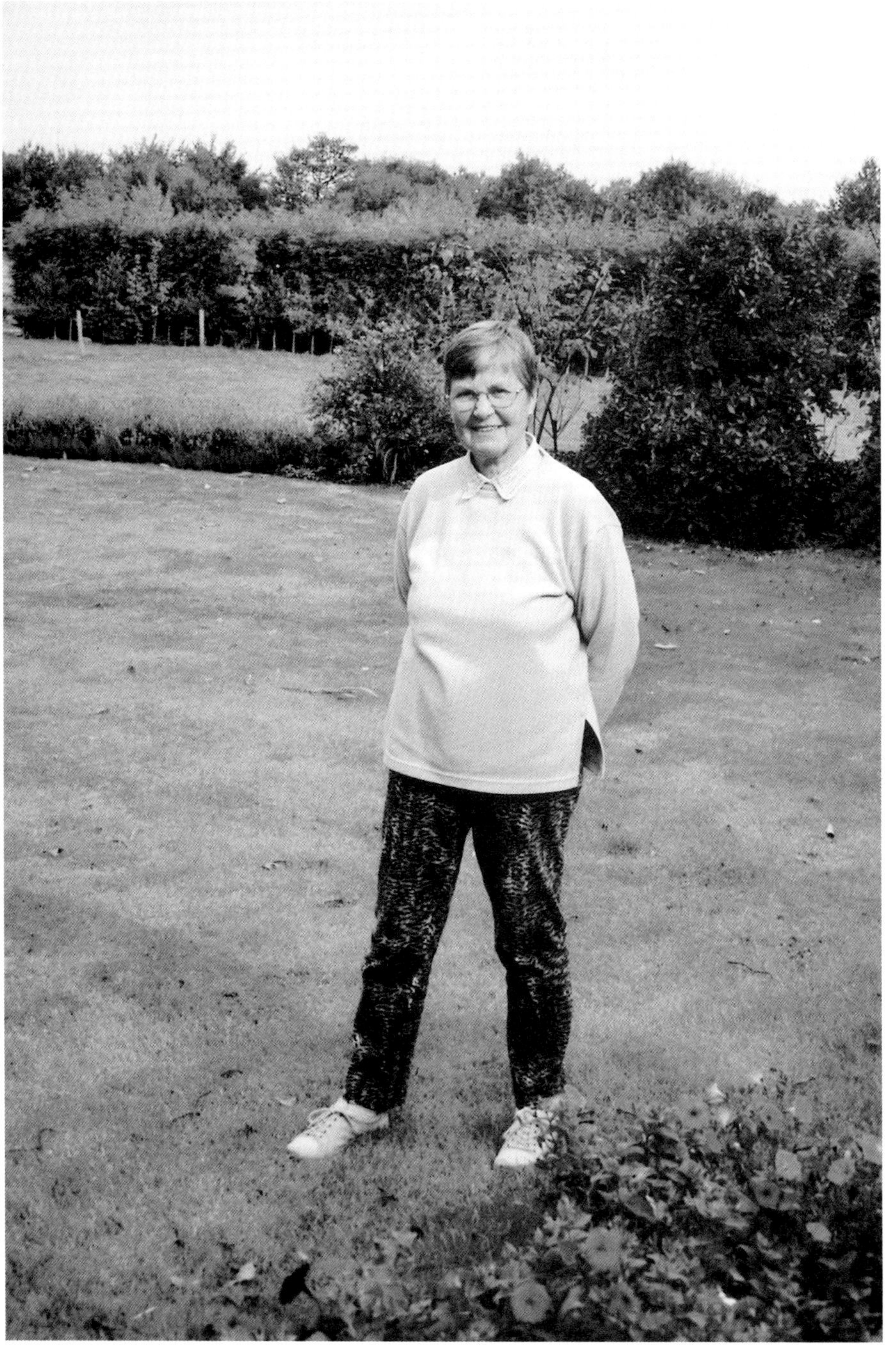

Diana Mansell

Jean and Diana's maternal grandfather, Alfred Berrill, a doctor/surgeon in South Woodford, Essex, discovered Burnham Overy Staithe around the turn of the 20th century. He rented Town House at the western edge of the Staithe, a name retained from its association with the parish poor house, pre the 1834 Union workhouse system. He enjoyed rabbit shooting on Scolt Island, with his springer spaniels, where there was, incredibly, a freshwater spring in the dunes. Knowledge of this oasis-like feature was passed down the family. Sadly with the constant coastal erosion, it was last detected on the foreshore in the 1960s/70s when their father was a member of the Nature Conservancy River Board.

Diana continues the story. "Grandmother Berrill, daughter of the vicar of Middleton, Yorks, was one of nine children. She inherited a bungalow, built of two railway carriages in the dunes on the west side of Gun Hill, on the death of her elder sister in 1916. Its brick fireplace and chimney breast are there to this day and form a favoured kestrel perch. Her youngest brother was an architect who left for Shanghai in 1903 and was subsequently caught up in all the horrors of the Japanese war. In happier times his favourite niece, Zoe Marion Berrill, sailed in February 1922 from Liverpool on one of the Blue Funnel Line steamers, to visit her uncle Bob Turner.

"The journey took a month, plenty of time to get acquainted with your fellow travellers, one of whom was R. C. Sherar, destined for Singapore on his return from leave with his family in Edinburgh. Roland Crichton Sherar, born in 1889, was the eldest of seven children of Edinburgh architect Robert F. Sherar. His maternal grandfather, John Crichton, and his elder brother, William, were in Sir Colin Campbell's famous 93rd Sutherland Highlanders Regiment at Balaclava in the Crimean War and formed part of the legendary 'thin red line tipped with steel' as later depicted by Robert Gibb.

"Roland was not destined for the drawing office and soon branched out on his own chosen pursuit of engineering. On completing a seven-year apprenticeship in Glasgow, he signed up with a company seeking skilled young men to operate their pioneering projects with tin mining and rubber planting, in the then Federated Malay States. He left Edinburgh in 1911 and having spent much of his spare time in Glasgow with the Volunteer Reserve

Army, he tried to enlist in 1914 but was turned down when found to have malaria. At the end of the war, many of the planters were sick and sent home on long overdue leave, whilst Roland Sherar was healthy and switched to the depleted ranks of rubber planters.

"His 1922 shipboard romance flourished at a distance and, in September, Zoe left Shanghai for Malaya and they were married in St Marks Church, Seremban, where they had a large, airy Company house. About this time Dad bought a plot of land on the coast at Port Dickson, adjacent to a small estate he ran in partnership with a fellow Scot. Our grandfather, in Edinburgh, designed the required bungalow which looked across the Malacca Straits. Endless white sands, lapped by crystal clear warm sea and with a jungle backdrop, made for an idyllic childhood playground. We had almost complete freedom, apart from certain strict rules that must always be adhered to. We were never to stand under a coconut tree without wearing a topee, and shoes were to be worn after dark to avoid large red centipedes and ferocious scorpions. I remember vividly finding one of the latter in my dolls' house – darkness came early and very swiftly.

"In the spring of 1933 Mum brought us home for schooling. I was approaching six and Jean was eight and a half. The only home we had was the bungalow on Overy beach, which had formed a quiet sanctuary during 'home leaves' and an escape from staying with one or other in-laws. This was Dad's introduction to Norfolk and

Jean and Diana

he decided to put Malaya 'on hold' and try his hand at farming whilst we were growing up. So many of our contemporary Brits abroad were brought up by grandparents and boarding school.

"Conveniently situated at the Staithe, was a little PNEU school for girls and little boys (pre prep). St Monica's was run by two Anglican nuns, of the Order of the Companions of the Good Shepherd of Wantage, who wore brown habit. The school was owned by Miss Mabel Grace Palmer whose father Samuel had been the maltster at Staithe House, later becoming the Moorings Hotel. She was a wonderful teacher and taught the older children, whilst Miss Ridewood concentrated on the 'babies'. I don't think we ever knew her Christian name; likewise there was a third nun who was only ever known as Companion Dorothea. I think she must have run the household. She was a dear soul, very kind and gentle, providing a hint of motherliness. Miss Palmer's elder sister, Esther Ada, lived in a house in New Road, to which her parents had earlier retired. She gave us piano lessons and was differentiated as Miss Barley Palmer after her little white terrier whom we all adored.

"The school was rapidly expanding in numbers in the 1930s and quite soon after we arrived a large wooden annexe was built in the garden providing sufficient floor space, when cleared, for our weekly dancing lessons. A Mrs Rutter used to come from Hunstanton, previously we had to go up the road to the old St Clement's parish room. The garden was large with many interesting mature trees, medlar, quince, mulberry, holm oak and an enormous cherry tree, exuding gum from its gnarled trunk. Beneath its vast spread was the main play area and I recall, vividly, the occasion in the summer of 1939 when a strange droning sound stopped us all in our tracks as we peered northwards at this gigantic silver, cigar shaped monster flying up the North Sea. Most of us had not seen more than a flimsy little bi-plane in the sky before and were filled with alarm. Subsequently I learned this was a Graf Zeppelin on a coastal mission identifying new radar defensive installations.

"We were greatly encouraged in all the arts. As well as lots of drawing and painting, needlework and music, we put on summer plays in the garden, to an audience of parents and the usual Christmas nativity.

"Meanwhile our mother moved to Hampshire to be near a cousin who would instruct her in chicken farming. She rented a house in Romsey which had a little Gothic shaped door in the wall, at the bottom of the back garden, opening directly onto the precincts of the great Norman abbey.

"Dad came home on leave that summer. We hadn't seen him since March and it took me a while to get used to his presence. In the late summer, before he was to depart again, I remember a walk in the Hampshire countryside and, on finding a thrush's nest full of speckled blue eggs, he set about impressing us with some of his boyhood enthusiasms, using Mum's brooch pin to pierce an egg which was highly addled, with disastrous consequences. Nevertheless this introduction paved the way for a future country pursuit and passion for all forms of nature.

"Dad was briefly home again in the summer of 1934, seriously seeking a suitable farm in the area. These were terrible slump years and farming was at a low ebb. The Burnham Westgate Hall Farm, of 100 acres, had been on the market for so long, without a buyer, that in desperation its perimeter had been drawn up as building plots. Fortunately only three plots had been sold and a fourth designated for a police house, when Dad had the rest reinstated as farmland and purchased for possession at Michaelmas 1934.

"The Hall had been presented to the Women's British Legion as a war memorial and the estate land was in the possession of George Robert Hudson, who had built himself a four-roomed bungalow out of some farm buildings he demolished. Dad sailed again for the East on October 6th to conclude his contract with the 3rd Mile Estate Rubber Co. and install a manager in his own estate, always hoping, one day, to return. Our poor mother was left to cope on her own, for eight and a half months, with a bungalow in the middle of a field, without running water or electricity and of course an outside loo, albeit attached.

Dad

"We girls became weekly boarders and relished this exciting new adventure. Mum acquired a maroon coloured bull-nosed Morris Cowley with a dickie seat. She was a skilled driver, having been in charge of a group of women driving a fleet of heavy army lorries in the WAACS. Dad had signed up a small labour force and bought some stock before leaving.

"Our pride and joy was Nellie, the Suffolk Punch, which he had bought at a farm sale and wondered why the old men were laughing at him. Nellie was

Nellie

lame having run a rusty nail into her hoof. Unperturbed and always the innovator, he equipped the stable with a syringe and left instructions for treating the wound which healed sufficiently for her to give many years of good service. She was rather prone to colic and on more than one occasion, Albert Francis, the foreman, would appear in the winter dark with Nellie in full harness and request Mum's aid while he went home for his tea. Explaining she had the belly ache and must not lie down, 'keep you a walking her around' would be the order. Albert lived in Mill Yard behind the Victoria pub and would get a bottle of ale, warm it, adding some potion which they would administer on his return. This task required pulling her head up on the halter via a pulley system over the hay rack, so that Albert could pour the mixture down her throat by standing on her trough, the whole evening's operation lit only by a hurricane lamp.

"The 1935 harvest was the only one we witnessed fully horse powered. Dad came home for good and soon set about utilising his engineering skills by introducing mechanised implements to Burnham. He started with a tractor and began ploughing up the old sheep pasture parkland, adding nearly 30 acres for crops. To bring in the hay he converted an old lorry chassis into a trailer, together with two shaftless wagons. The three vehicles hitched

Implements

together presented a motley spectacle rattling along the farm roads. The stack building was economised further by rigging up a primitive diesel engine to operate the elevator's horse gin. With Dad home we became day girls and soon learned to ride bikes and propelled ourselves to school in Overy.

"Meanwhile grandfather Sherar had drawn up plans for a new gable wing extension with typical 1930s curved Crittal-window architecture and the use of modern reinforced concrete walls, a feature later builders found problematic on their pneumatic drills! Two 'brickies' and a 'chippie', under the strict eye of the gaffer, had to repeat anything that wasn't 'spot on'. The building process was patiently borne by Mum but referred to as 'Henry little by little'. The first move was making use of the bungalow's roof space and for some time Jean and I retired by ladder.

"One end of the barn, too, had been given an upper floor to provide a workshop full of lathes and pulleys, entered from outside through a window. Underneath were rows of glass batteries which supplied our own electricity: not a very bright light and one that dimmed every time another was switched on, so when we went to bed the call, 'How many lights have you got on up there?' invariably followed. The pump-up paraffin lamps, with their flimsy filaments, were mothballed and hung along the back corridor – in case! Of course the power for cooking, ironing and hoovering was not provided on this system. I think it was the early 1950s before mains electricity came our way.

"In spite of all the building upheaval, Mum seemed able to find room for guests. She was a sort of surrogate mother to friends whose parents were still abroad. In the summer holidays she shipped us all down to the beach bungalow whose two railway carriages provided four single and two double bedrooms. The endless dunes, sea bathing and mudlarking in the marsh dykes, with rafts made from an abundance of flotsam and jetsam, kept us happy. Very high tides were fabulous fun providing a vast swimming pool almost from the doorstep, the submerged foot bridges that spanned the main dykes had hand rails which made excellent diving boards.

"Mum was also a staunch supporter of the WI in the years when most of its members were true villagers and Wednesday afternoons were fully half-day closing. She was their President for over 12 years.

Jean, Diana and friends

"The other commodity Dad engineered to the house was running water and of course flush loos. Beside the horse trough in the upper yard was a well and hand pump which went deep into the chalk. Alongside was a shed that was made into a pump house in which a 2000 gallon brick tank was constructed and kept full of reserve water in case of fire, delicious as drinking water but it almost abrased the skin and made your hair stand on end. So hair washing entailed filling every available pan from the big rain butt to heat up on the Raeburn, after first sieving off the mosquito larvae. An electric pump was installed into the well and pumped water directly up to the house.

"In about 1936/7 he bought the Hawker's Hill farm and house – two men had been living there who had a contract for collecting and disposing of all Burnham's waste including the night cart. On the summit of the hill, west of Hawker's Hill wood, was a marl pit into which all the tins, glass and stoneware container jars were thrown, providing us with another happy hunting ground, never suspecting that much of this bounty underfoot would become collectors' items.

" I'm afraid that Codd's mineral water bottles were prized for their imprisoned glass marble in the neck. However I do pride myself for having been attracted to a 16th century stoneware container for wine before the era of glass bottles. Some 35 years later, my own boys revelled in the hidden and overgrown magic, seeking out the beauty of tears and streaks, blob tops or sheared lips, embossed beers and medicines, together with a whole new interest in social history.

"About this time, Dad purchased his first combine harvester, a second-hand American International harvester with an 8 foot cut and still drawn by tractor. I remember the excitement when we were all packed into the big old Austin to go to see his next prized machine, somewhere near Grantham. To my amazement we stopped beside a field gateway and inside was what looked like a heap of rusting old iron. I couldn't believe this was what we had come all this way to see. Dad had it transported to Hawker's Hill and installed in the barn. It was Burnham's first corn drier.

" To many of the local farming fraternity, Dad was still a 'furriner' and a bit of a madman with his newfangled ideas. The harvest of 1938 was a very wet one and the early cut corn began sprouting green in the stooks or shocks. Meanwhile the 'madman's' corn was still standing uncut until it was ripe and he cut it with an audience looking over the Whiteway Road gate, already threshed into sacks and whisked away to the drier. Old Philip Roy approached Dad and asked, 'Well wha' d'yew call thet thare contrapshun, then?' By the early 1940s the Roy farms had introduced combines. Hancocks at Norton held out until after the war. These were the small beginnings of a vast implement industry that engulfs the region today.

"In 1939, just as war was declared, Jean and I moved on to Dereham High School. It was predominantly a day school with a catchment area including Swaffham, Shipdham and Wymondham on the rail network. The headmistress had a large house facing the Market Square with an extensive annexe at the rear, originally a First World War army billet, the whole complex surrounded by a large walled garden with a tennis court. Here some 30 of us boarded under somewhat spartan conditions. After taking Cambridge school certificate two years later, Jean moved on to drama school in Edinburgh and London prior to joining the WRNS. As a signaller she was stationed on the Isle of Wight during the Normandy invasion and involved in semaphoring the troops across the Channel. She ended her service having a pretty good time in Alexandria.

"Periodically, the Head would come round the dorms painting our throats with gentian violet, which coincided, one fateful night, with one of our more risky escapades. Two of the seniors would take orders for a pennyworth or two of chips. They would shin up the pear tree against the kitchen garden wall and climb down the cattle pens the other side and across the Market Place to the fish and chip shop. There were no plastic carriers in those days. Presumably they were just wrapped in newspaper. The junior dorm had just been distributed with their share of the bounty when Miss G. came on her rounds complete with her old ginger spaniel. She went round with her tongue in her cheek while the spaniel rooted around under our beds pulling at the newspaper. Then she instructed one of us to collect all the packages in an enamel basin and they were confiscated. Next day, at a more appropriate time, they were served up to us cold. I don't think it stopped the chip run completely.

"After three years in the boarding house, being seriously ill on two occasions but not wanting to leave the school, I spent my final two years very happily in digs in the town. I became a day girl and cycled to school with a completely different set of friends. The pecking order amongst the different categories was horrendous – boarders, day girls, train girls. My landlady took her new responsibilities very seriously. Much of the breakfast room was filled by the huge Morrison table shelter, heaped underneath with layers of feather mattresses on which her elderly spaniel spent most of its time sleeping.

"There were frequent air raids on Norwich about 16 miles distant and from my east facing window I had a grand view of the fireglow lighting the night sky. Shortly before D Day and fortunately for me the school was hit by incendiary bombs aimed at the railway trucks nearby, loaded with ammunition for the forthcoming battles. The next morning there were still some in the playground trees and we had the day off. Neither I nor my parents knew that Dereham was equipped with a bomb factory.

"After School Certificate I went to the Edinburgh College of Art to fill a year before becoming eligible to join the WAAFS. Fortunately the war in Europe ended the following May and I stayed on for the whole four-year Diploma Course, two years general and two years specialising in typography and book illustration, graduating in June 1948. That autumn I began my teacher training at Moray House College of Education for a year, experiencing some pretty varied ages and class conditions during my student teaching, from the primary tots in a lowly area near Holyrood Palace, whom I found difficult to comprehend, via the rather snooty girls' grammar school where the staff sat in breathing down your neck with an air of disapproval, to finally a large secondary school in the Leith docks area. Here, in contrast, the staff evaporated to their staff room on seeing the arrival of their student replacement.

"My usual class were 15-year-old girls about to leave school. On enquiring whether they were permitted to come in curlers and headscarves the reply in chorus was, 'Please Miss, we're goin' jiggin' the neet.' I was supposed to keep them occupied all afternoons on some useless formula and a piece of paper six by eight inches. In a matter of five minutes they were up on the cupboards below the roller blackboard, all set out with evening class algebra which they began smudging out. Confronted with this row of bare calfs was too tempting and I slapped my hand along the whole line; they came down like a pack of cards. After that I got them designing the contents of the sort of homes they would quite soon be setting up for themselves and we became firm friends.

"I stuck my neck out applying for art school posts and received a stream of negative replies. Eventually I was summoned to appear before the Board of Interviewers at the Shire Hall in Hereford where there were two vacancies at the little Art School. One was for drawing and painting with pottery, and the other design and crafts. I was applying for the latter with weaving and silversmithing my main crafts. The little Art School was in a beautiful Queen Ann house on the banks of the river Wye. My design room on the first floor had a large bay window overhanging the river. On a tranquil day you could watch pike quivering in the shallows, but after heavy rain and storms in the mountains, its mood changed to violent ochrous rapids hurtling trees and dead sheep in its passage.

"After a brief spell in a bedsit I moved into a spacious flat in Town with my new colleague. We took students on cheap rail excursions to London to visit museums and galleries and sometimes the ballet. After three years I began to think it was time to move on and try to get into publishing in London. It took until the summer of 1953 before the new principal agreed to replace me. I spent two or three months at home working up a portfolio, my father constantly reminding me he couldn't understand why I had given up a perfectly good job.

"So I packed my bags and headed for London and settled into a draughty north-facing bedsit in Hampstead, with a gas meter that devoured shillings with a voracious appetite. I had a friend nearby who had opted out of Moray House and was working at Adprint in Rathbone Place.

They printed some cheap American children's books which I worked on freelance, drawing out each colour on overlay film. It was tedious but helped to feed the meter. Later they employed a huge workforce in their basement, mainly out-of-work actors and actresses, constructing pop-up books, paid piece rate.

"We all worked so hard that we finished short of Christmas, so with a new actress friend I set out to find sales work in the stores. We were taken on by Bourne and Hollingsworth where I worked in the semi-basement book department. It was astonishing that businessmen would come in during their lunch hour and request suitable books for specific age groups and interests and leave with a stack of books two feet high, all chosen by 'you'.

"The following spring I got a post with Phoenix House in a gorgeous little Regency building sandwiched into William IV Street. It was a subsidiary of Dents under its own director. We handled no fiction, concentrating on biography, history, archaeology and the arts. We also ran a print gallery on the ground floor and three book clubs: Readers Union, The Country and Sportsman, and I got to do the first art work for the whole House – some 60 jackets a year and all the advertising brochures for the gallery and clubs. Being such a small outfit there was a very friendly atmosphere. One of our lunchtime haunts was a marvellous pub in Covent Garden, frequented by market porters, which served homestyle meals at a very low price.

"Gradually we girls got married and left to bring up our families; which led to a strange coincidence reviving the past. A particular friend, whose son was slightly older than mine, rang me one day from her doctor/friend's house. She was being shown an autograph album in which she found mine and my sister's names. The album's owner was Mabel Grace Palmer. It transpired that the doctor was her great-nephew, Graham Cassels-Brown, with whom she was shortly coming to stay. And so it was on a sweltering day in July 1959 at a children's birthday party in Twickenham, I was able to meet again after 20 years, Sister Mabel Grace, as she had become. Looking exactly the same, with her little polished apple cheeks enveloped by her starched veil lining. That was to be my lasting memory of her.

"On that same hot summer day, 31st July 1959, the water mill at Burnham Overy Staithe became a blazing inferno. It had been purchased by the National Trust in 1939 from Sidney Everitt who retired that September and Dad became the first Trust tenant. He also bought up a number of marshes belonging to smallholders. During the 1940s he drained the marshes; some still had ancient horseshoe shaped clay drainpipe systems, imprinted with 'drain 1825' to avoid tax duty. He converted the hackney stable at the yard entrance into an electrified milking parlour in readiness for his proposed TT Jersey herd.

"After the war he began visiting the Channel Isles and buying hand picked cows from different locations. In the Islands there are no herds, the cows are pegged on halters; these were the progenitors of the beautiful Mill herd which Dad gradually built up. The old matriarchs all had fancy French names and sounded quite funny being called by the local cowmen. In the early 1950s he decided to open up another dairy, building a milking parlour in the old stables at Hall Farm – today it is a private kitchen. Sadly, the terrible North Sea surge on the last night of January 1953 scuppered his plans. The mill was inundated with water and something like 18 little heifer calves instantly drowned. With the courageous help of John Green from the Mill House, in freezing water, they were able to release older heifers from their halters, having to force their heads under water to do so. The herd remained at Overy and John Smith took over in 1971.

"Dad never returned to Malaya and sold out in the 1950s, disenchanted with the Communist powers surrounding the country he had loved. When he died at Christmas 1990 he was in his 102nd year.

"I got hooked on genealogy in the 1970s, just at a time when record offices and family history societies were emerging county by county. We had built 'Wildwood' in 1965 and I spent much of the boys' school holidays here. I saw the Burnhams in a different light and began asking numerous questions to which there was no easy way of finding the answers, so I began delving myself. I discovered too, that there were no full transcripts of the parish registers and all except Burnham Norton were kept in the churches. I persuaded the rector, Cecil Isaacson, to let me transcribe them, which I did throughout the 1980s. Many people have done odd researches from time to time but their findings never seem to be available. I want the Burnhams to have an archive that can be handed down to posterity. Today's modern processes make this more and more attainable. I have built up a black and white photographic record of the 20th century which is ongoing whenever people lend me something of interest. But we do need a new village hall with space to house it. And a village undivided.

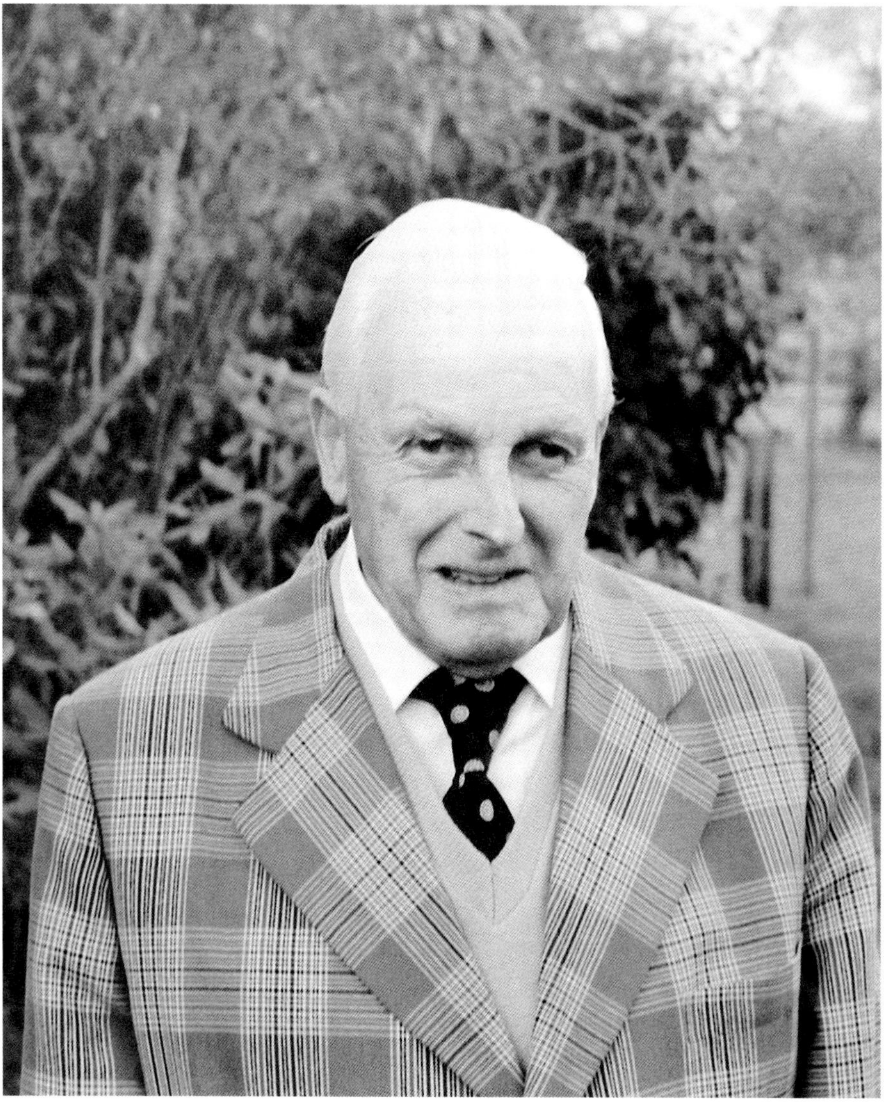

Jimmy Rout

Jimmy Rout was born in 1921 in Rogers Row, Station Road, Burnham Market, one of seven children of William and Sarah Rout. Jimmy's brothers were Charles, Robert, Lawrence (always known as Joe) and John. He had two sisters – Mary and May.

Jimmy continues: "I have a photo of the Burnham School 'baby' band, in which I played the triangle, performing at St Andrews Hall, Norwich, in 1928. I kept out of trouble at school and was never caned by Mr Keeble or Mr Newell. I was average as a pupil and did not much take to sport. The cricket ball was too hard and in football you got kicked." Jimmy Rout's philosophy of keeping out of trouble helped to ensure his survival as a prisoner of war of the Japanese, for three and a half years, in the Second World War.

"When I left school, aged 14, in 1935, there was no work to be had, so I spent a year buying and selling wild rabbit skins. Depending on their size and quality they would fetch fivepence to eightpence and I would pay the supplier – usually a farmer twopence or more per skin. At the age of 15 I got a job at Crow Hall Farm, where there were some 12 to 15 men employed.

"I joined the Territorial Army in 1938, along with 23 others. We were all recruited on one day in St Edmunds Room. Captain Lance from Norton was in command, and we had to pass a medical before we could sign up. I can remember names of 22 of us who were called up on the same day, although most of them are no longer with us. In addition to me, there was my brother-in-law to be, Ronnie Bottomley, Cyril, Charles and Fred Woodhouse, Jack and Arthur Parsons who worked for Bickell Builders, and Arnold Cousins. Also, Sid, Billy and Bob Scoles and S. Scoles, D. and H. Hall, G. Rout, G. Barwick, W. Codman, L. Chilvers, M. Flowerdew, G. Snell, E. Warnes and R. Havers.

"Leslie Harvey had a car and three or four of us shared all sorts of enjoyable adventures with him, and went to Norwich every Saturday. We were never sure how a car journey was going to end. On occasion the lights would give up and we would have to stop frequently to charge the batteries. If it wasn't the lights it was the brakes, or a tyre would blow. Leslie taught the lads to drive, and it is one of my regrets that I never took my driving test because I was so involved with the Territorial Reserves. As it has turned out, it is as much as I can do to find a parking space for my bicycle in Burnham Market these days.

"Having signed up to the Territorials, we were sent to camp at Falmouth for two weeks training, and thereafter trained once a week at Dersingham. It was different, a break from our routine lives, and there was good comradeship. When war was declared in 1939 we were called up immediately into the 7th Royal Norfolks. Then the two or three of us who were not old enough were transferred to the 5th Royal Norfolks and sent to Cranwich near Thetford. From there we went to North Walsham for just one night, before being redeployed to West Raynham airfield to guard a bomb dump. We did this for five or six weeks until we were moved to Weybourne for training. Then to Holt and on to West Beckham to guard the radar installation there. Then back to Holt and Weybourne again, until we were sent to King's Lynn to guard the docks at Estuary Point. After a few weeks we were sent to Cheshire to Marbury Hall, near Northwich. It was harvest time and those of us who were interested set to work in the fields.

"Our next stop was Scotland, where we were prepared for posting abroad. We were quite philosophical about our lot. After all we had signed up as volunteers and were ready to do whatever was asked of us. We embarked on the SS *Duchess of Atholl*, which we soon named the 'Drunken Duchess' as it pitched and rolled across the Atlantic, bound for Halifax in Canada. There we were transferred to the *Mount Vernon*, an enormous liner, with so many holds it took weeks to find our way around. It was one of three ships in a convoy which was to take us 13 weeks to steam to Singapore via Mombasa. We encountered no U boats and thought that, either we were going on an extended route to avoid them, or the powers that be did not know where to send us, which is why it took so long.

"After disembarking at Singapore we headed up through Malaya to face the Japanese, whom we knew were coming down towards Singapore. But we strayed too far up and, with the help of guides and every man for himself, we were guided to boats and taken back to Singapore. Once there, the Causeway, which links it to Malaya, was blown up. Nonetheless, the Japanese poured through. The game was up. Our commanding officer was Major Harry Schumann from Creake, and he ordered us to surrender. He tied a white flag to the end of a rifle and rode towards the invading army on a ladies, bike. 'We've had it boys,' he said, 'put your hands up and hope for the best.' Major Schumann still lives in South Creake.

" The Japanese surrounded us and told us to put our watches, rings and any other valuables on the ground in front of us. Then they came and helped themselves. However when a Japanese officer appeared he lined up all the guards who had stolen our belongings, took his sword from his belt, but still in its scabbard, and clouted each of the Japanese responsible. He then commanded them to return the valuables to the ground again, and they were restored to us. It was a lesson that the Japanese could be just as harsh with their own people as with their prisoners if they or we had done something wrong.

"We were set to building a prisoner of war camp, and had to learn our numbers in Japanese. They didn't speak English, and certainly didn't speak Norfolk. My number was 178 and I can still say it in Japanese. They sorted us out for different destinations and we walked to Changi barracks near the coast. This was situated at the far end of the infamous Changi jail. Once there, a number of our troops were sent to work on the Burma railway. These included Fred Woodhouse who survived and returned after the war to work on the railways in Norfolk. We came home together and he was best man at my wedding to Joan in 1946. He died of a heart attack when riding his bicycle about three years ago.

"I was in the contingent that was sent to Japan, where we worked in quarries, carbine factories and metal working. If we behaved we were reasonably treated. There were a few nervous young guards who walked around with pick handles and few words. They were more unpredictable than the older ones, but the latter were always being transferred to fight at the front. We had adequate rations of rice, and when that ran out, we were given millet or rye. The Japanese people ate the same and were very hungry towards the end.

" We were allowed to hold a church service every Sunday evening, and the Japanese guards were instructed to stay at a distance, so as not to intrude upon the worship. One of our officers had made a radio set from scrap parts, but he needed an aerial. I was on the top bunk of the sleeping block, and the chosen spot for the aerial was the washing line attached to my bunk. The officer had warned us that we all faced death if we were caught. I always kept laundry hanging on the line. We listened to the news, and the Sunday evening sermon took the form of an update of that news to the congregation. The radio was never discovered.

"When the Burma Railway was completed, there was an influx of prisoners to our camp. There was plenty of room, for although there had been 1000 of us in that camp originally, deaths from berri berri and dysentery had thinned out the numbers. It always seemed to be the big strong prisoners who died. Maybe they had not had the tough upbringing we had had in Norfolk, and could not take the hardships we all endured. Until the new intake arrived, there had been only one Norfolkman in the camp, but another seven arrived at that time, including Fred Woodhouse. There was a heavy snow fall one winter, and we had to get onto the roof of the buildings, which were flimsily built, and clear it.

"We knew the war was coming to an end, through our radio. The Allies started dropping food and medicines by parachute, in and around the camp. We were allowed out in small numbers, and under guard, to retrieve them. The atom bombs had fallen on Hiroshima and Nagasaki, but there was no information on that on the radio. The end came, and the Japanese escorted us by train to Tokyo. Then the Americans took us to Okinawa by plane, to fatten us up in preparation for the journey home. We spent 10 days in Manila in the Philippines, before leaving by boat for Victoria in British Colombia, Canada. We were fumigated, showered, given a medical and fitted out with new uniforms. Everything we had been wearing was incinerated. My only ailment was leg ulcers from which most of us suffered. They took time to heal and I still have the scars.

"After two weeks we left by train to cross Canada. It took a week, and we stopped for 20 minutes at every station, where the local people plied us with food and particularly chocolate, which we had not tasted for three and a half years. We reached Halifax. I had come full circle. We embarked on a French liner for Portsmouth which we entered quietly in 1945. All countries are the same in war. We travelled by train to King's Lynn. Cataleuhs, the King's Lynn outfitters, arranged transport for us back to Burnham. They were a famous, if pricey, firm in King's Lynn. Their clothes were reputed to be of good quality, and if you were found in the rain without a coat, you would be asked. 'Got a Cataleuh jacket on – dear?'

"We were still in uniform until we were called, two or three weeks later, to Northampton, for demob. We were given a set of civilian clothes and our back pay – mine was about £100!

"When I returned home, I found that my brother John had died on the operating table, whilst a prisoner of war of the Germans. My family had all married and I set about the same course. Mother had never locked the door of our house, day or night, while we were away at the war. In the hope that we might return at any time, she did not want us to find the door locked so we could not get into our own home. Even though we lived next door to Jack Marsh on the Sutton Estate, she did not worry about anyone getting into the house because she had a little terrier who would allow no one to pass. He was as good as the stoutest lock.

"Employers had to take you back on demob, and keep you for a while at least, even if they wanted to get rid of you. I resumed at Crowhall Farm, where I stayed until Joan and I married in 1946. We then went to live for eight years at Muckleton, where I worked, and then in 1954 we moved into a council house. I worked for the Roys for many years at Crowhall and Friarthorne farms, until I retired. A truck from 'HQ' used to pick us up in the middle of the village at 7 a.m and drop us there at 4 p.m. I worked a horse at Friarthorne for many years to cart cattle feed.

"I had met Joan Bottomley when she lived with her parents at Thorpe Road Gatehouse, where her father was the railway gatekeeper. Her parents moved to Station Road in Burnham in October 1943. The trains had stopped on May 31st 1952. Joan was born in 1923. We were engaged for a few months and then married at Sutton Church. We had six children, three of each, and Joan would walk from Muckleton to the village to shop, every Friday, and she would visit her

Jimmy and Joan

parents in Station Road. The children are all married and we have 14 grandchildren and seven great grandchildren.

"Our son Raymond lives in New Zealand, and we went out to see him in 1981. On the way back we stopped off at Singapore and saw the Changi jail and barracks. Raymond has been over here a couple of times. He was in the Royal Navy on HMS *Eagle*, before being accepted for service on the Royal Yacht, *Britannia*. He served as a steward and then leading steward altogether for seven years and then signed on for a few more months, until it reached New Zealand, where he met the girl he married. When *Britannia* was to be decommissioned he was invited to the ceremony and flew to Britain where he met members of the Royal Family once again.

"We have a daughter living in South Creake, and we see her and her family two or three times a week. Our two other daughters live near Norwich and our youngest son, Tony Rout the builder, lives in Docking. Sadly John, our eldest son died in 1989.

"The changes in Burnham Market, over the last 20 years, have been good for traders, but have put great pressure on the village we have known all our lives. Something needs to be done about the traffic, and the very least is that Front Street and North Street should both be made one way." After living here for 82 years Jimmy speaks with feeling.

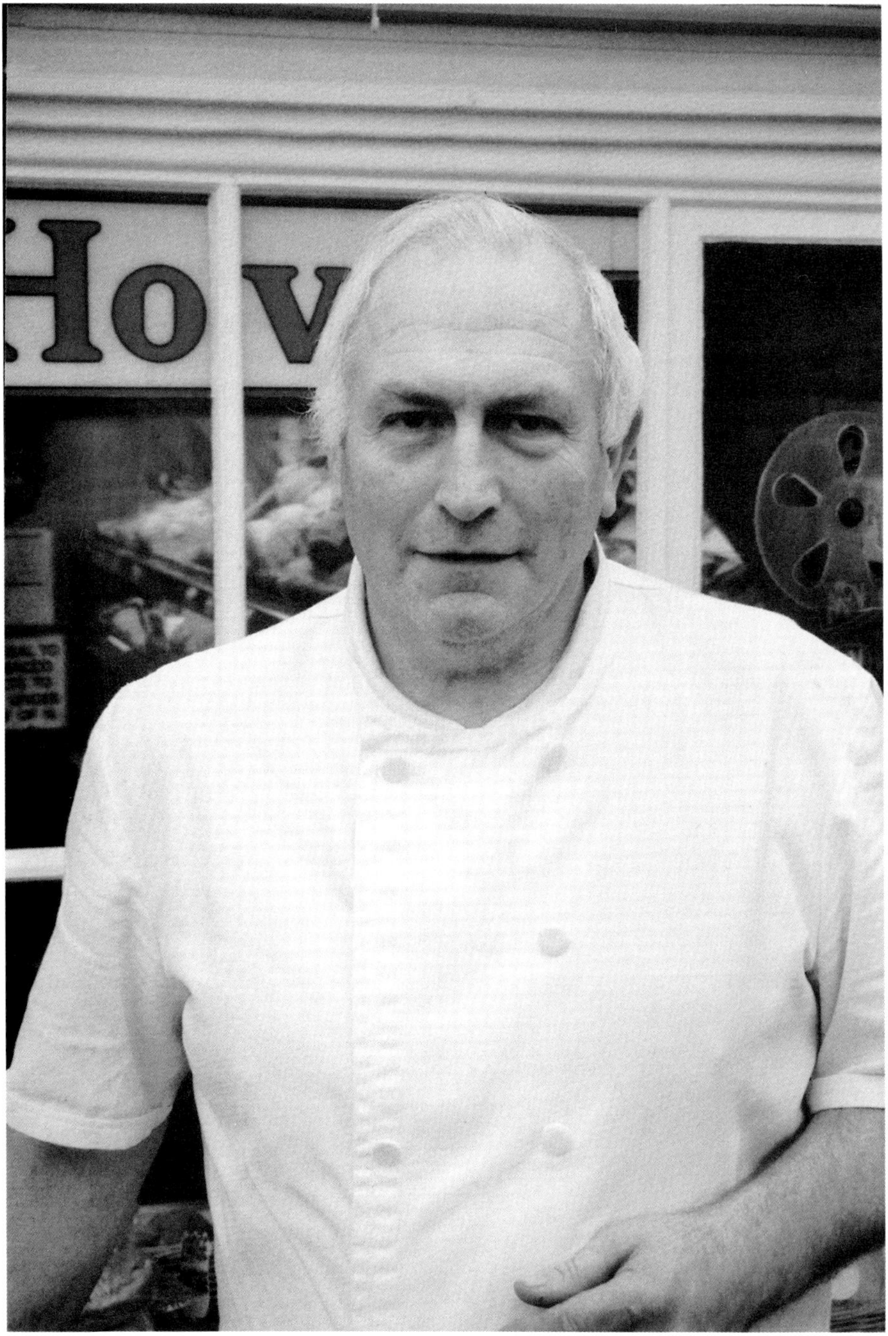

Peter Groom

Peter Groom's grandfather, Arthur Groom, came to Burnham Market from Terrington St Clement in 1925 and worked for Hammonds Bakery for two years. He then set up on his own in the bakery and shop which continues the Grooms' tradition today. He was later joined by Peter's father, and they lived where Gurneys fish shop is today. "My father later set up his own bakery, in rented premises, in Brancaster, before returning to Burnham Market in 1957, following my grandfather's death the year before." Peter Groom, and his elder brother, John, were born in Brancaster in 1945 and 1943 respectively.

"My parents had met in Overy Staithe. My mother to be was nanny to the family of the Revd Wallace, who lived at Hainford and had a holiday home in one of the beach huts in Overy Staithe. When Mother went back to Hainford, my father cycled 42 miles each way to see her. They courted for four years before they married, and Mother, who lived to be 90, died four years ago.

"I left school at 15 wanting to go into the Royal Navy, but my father had a heart attack, two years after I left school, and needed my help in the business. I have no regrets. My mother, who was a great cook, taught me to make cakes. I sang in the Westgate Church choir. There were seven of us, and we were tormented, in a moderately kindly sort of way, by Mr Irvine who was in his 60s, lived in Front Street and was a senior member of the choir. He would clip us playfully about the ears and make remarks. He would carry the torment to the cricket field, where he watched us play, and shouted abuse. He probably thought he was funny but we did not share that opinion. I was part of the gang of boys who drove cattle from the market to the railway to be shipped out by train. We would also help Mr Barker to pull the cattle down to be slaughtered and we would boil the pigs to rid them of their hair.

"Among the characters in those days were Mr Allen, Reggie Baldry's uncle, who owned a cobblers shop and fruit shop in Julers Yard in Front Street. Then there was Miss Pike, and her sister, who lived in Estcourt House. She made her front room available for the visiting dentist on Sunday mornings. She had been a teacher at Stanhoe and ended her days in Brett House in Overy Staithe. She was interested to the last in how Burnham Market had got on at football and cricket. She always knew the Test match scores, and it is reported that, on her 100th birthday, she received a telegram of congratulations from Norwich City Football Club.

"Grooms is the longest established business in Burnham Market. Stymans ran us close as did West Norfolk Radio set up by Ernie Utting three years after my grandfather started Grooms bakery. Before 1927 the Grooms shop was a combined sweets and cycle shop, called Nurse, and I have a picture of it. My grandfather installed peel ovens when he converted it into a bakery and these were heated with faggots.

"They were set alight in the oven and scuffled out before the bread was baked. These gave way to coal, and then to oil, which was fed into the oven along a long burner. Today our six deck ovens are fired by electricity, and while this is much cleaner, the best fuel was coal – it was dirty to work with but it gave off a marvellous heat.

"The bakery workers used to sleep, at night, on the top of the dough troughs, and when the dough rose sufficiently it tipped them off and it was time to make the bread. One of the longest serving was Ray Petts, who left us, for a while, to work at the West End Bakery in Wells, but came back and stayed until retirement.

"The equipment we installed in the early years was amazingly reliable. We had a Dumbril mixer which was secondhand when we bought it in the

Second World War and had had one breakdown, in 1960, when a fibre cob went. I thought it would put paid to the machine and not even Ernie Utting or John Utting would have a replacement! But we contacted Dumbrils on the phone and within 10 minutes they had found the records of the machine number, the date of its installation and how and when we paid for it. The replacement was here next day.

"We decided to include speciality breads in our range such as sunflower, cheese and onion and rye. This was going well until our flour supplier started competing with his customers by opening bakery shops, thus forcing the closure of many small bakers. We had to find another source of supply. We located John Here, the specialist flour producer, restored the three specialities and developed another nine. We run one or two each day. We have built up a prestige catering clientele including many of the favoured eating places in the district."

Peter Groom starts work each weekday at 3 a.m and at 2 a.m at the weekend. He and John James light up the ovens and prepare the doughs. The first bread is baked by 4.30 a.m and the day's requirements are ready for the shop to open at 9 a.m. His catering customers want their rolls and morning goods in time for their breakfast service. Some days, when there is a particularly heavy demand, Grooms make another batch, providing they know by 11.45 a.m so that it can be ready for sale at 1.15 p.m.

Despite these unsocial hours and the need for some sleep – Peter says he can sleep anywhere at anytime – he plays an active part in the life of the village. He is one of the founder members of the Burnham Traders who meet two or three times a year, unless there is a pressing reason for additional meetings. They plan the stunning Christmas lights which draw visitors from many miles away. The Traders started in a pub.

"I was elected to the Parish Council 25 years ago, at the same time as Steven Andrews of Ulf Draperies, who now lives in Hunstanton. I have been vice chairman for 10 years and believe I have a role to speak out about controversial issues affecting the village.

"I played badminton in the winter for many years. My friend Ernie Hammond died at 51 after a game in which he played his heart out. It was a terrible shock when he dropped dead after the match. I shredded my achilles tendon and had to give up the game. I then turned my attention to the playing field, and was chairman of the committee for 10 years. We had no money until we offered the field for parking during the craft fair. The first year we made

£900. We set to work to level the field and this meant closing it for play for two years. The football and cricket clubs moved to Thorpe for that period. We constructed tennis courts for the first time."

Peter played cricket for many years for Burnham Market until the late 1970s. He was opening bat with a highest score of 90+ and a spin bowler. "I played with such skilled team mates as Cyril Nice and Robin Nice. George Sutherland, the station master at Burnham Market, recorded the longest boundary six in history. He hefted the ball from the pavilion end and it landed up in Docking. It was helped on its way by a moving goods train, but it was no mean feat to get it as far as the train.

"I had a Morris Traveller in the 1970s and was the only member of the team with a car. On one occasion, the whole team plus the kit and the umpire crammed into the car and we drove to Creake. The first car we passed was a police car. The police came to see me the following day, to say that they had dreamt they had seen a complete cricket team in a Morris Traveller – and don't do it again. From then on we went in two cars.

"The farms employed enough men from which to draw at least one cricket team. Herbert Kendal and his four sons were all good cricketers. He was captain of the Burnham second team before joining Stilgoe's team. He expected all the players to do well and, if they did not, the whole village would hear about it. We were all passionate about the game and played in the Sandringham League. Sometimes I played five nights a week, doing the rounds at Deepdale, Holkham, Thorpe, Docking and North Creake.

"Digger Rust was a farm foreman from Norton and a keen cricketer. I was innocent, in those days, and really believed that the young ladies he was pledged to their parents to see home, were indeed his nieces. I found it hard to understand how he had so many. When he offered me a lift home, he would drop me at a pub for a while, so that he could escort a young 'niece' lady to her home. Sometimes I was in for a long wait before he returned to continue our journey home. He was driving a number of us, on one occasion, to a match at Wrack Heath, when he had a sneezing fit as he approached a busy main road. He put his foot on the accelerator, instead of the brake, and we shot across the road between the crossing traffic. An irate driver stormed up and berated Digger. The scene looked ugly, and then the police arrived. Digger was still sneezing helplessly and the police were more sympathetic at the state of him, than the motorist. It's a wonder we all escaped a car smash.

"I was a keen sailor in my fireball, although my boat seemed to spend sufficient time upside down in the water to earn it the name PG Tips. After I sold it I sailed for many years with Timmy Roy at Brancaster in a 505. We won most of the cups available. I gave up, 10 years ago, when I shredded my achilles tendon. I have also been keen at bowls and, for many years, I was a member of the club which got to the finals of the county cup six years running.

"When we had the last big freeze, and snow drifts made it impossible to travel other than by tractor to deliver supplies, Dick Battersby and I set out with a load of bread and ended up completely sozzled on tea. I would not have thought that possible but then I was unaware, when we started out, what fortification the kind and grateful customers had put into the tea. We were past caring on the way home, and took the shortest route. When the snow had melted Mr Hancock called on my father and told him he had something to show him. He took him to a 12 foot hedge, with two sets of tractor treads across the top of it, and this is where we had driven in the snow, unworried at any possible consequences on the other side of the hedge. We had sobered up by that time, and had no difficulty in assuring him that we would not repeat the experience.

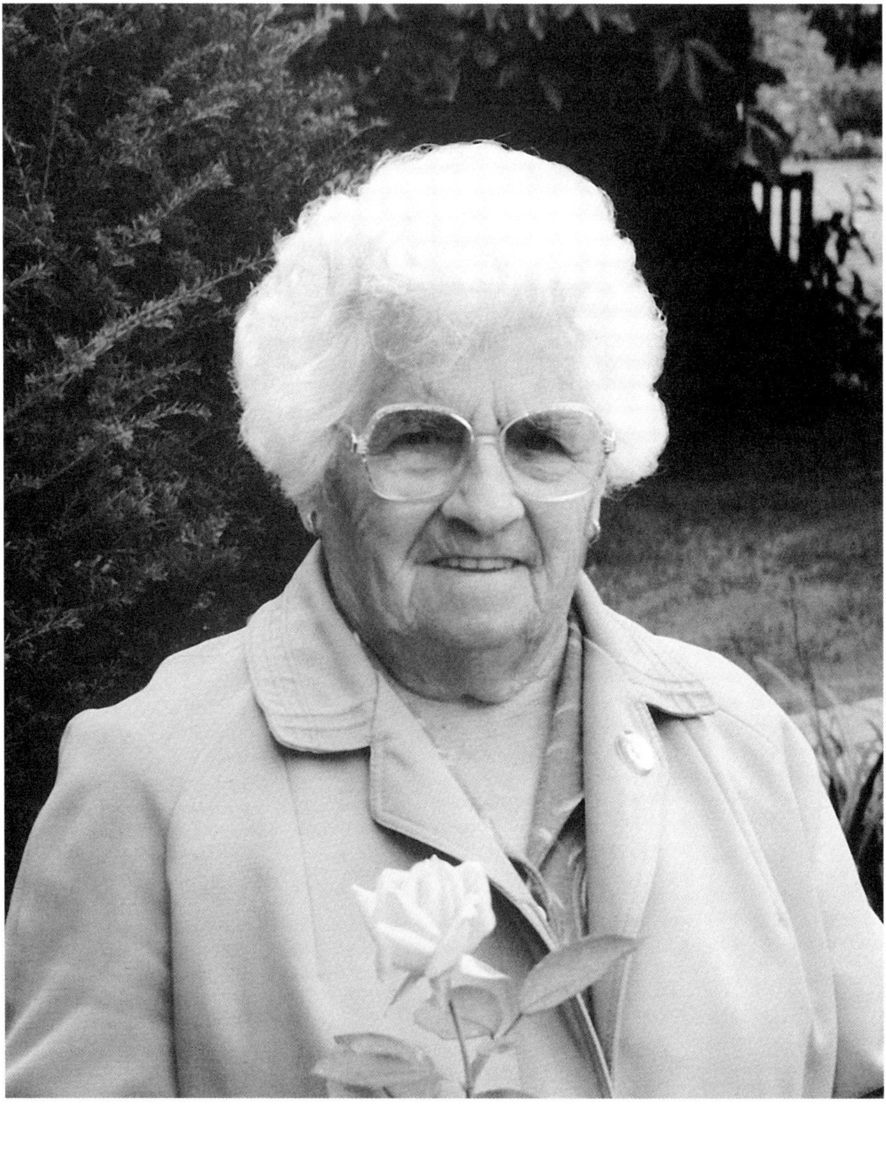

Annie Franklin

Annie Horney was born in Little Dunham near Litcham in 1915. She had two brothers and three sisters. Her father was in the Royal Navy during the whole of the First World War. Early tragedy struck when her brother aged three and a half was knocked down and killed by a milk cart as he ran into the road. Her other brother went on to join the Royal Navy in the Second World War where he was wounded and two ships were sunk under him.

"We left school at 14 in those days although I never managed to finish my last term as I was in hospital with an abscess on the lung. I still have a large scar from the operation to this day. It is possible to make out all the stitches – very different from the keyhole surgery one has these days. I really enjoyed school and was good at most things. They taught us useful things. For example, we had a term learning laundry, and another housewivery, and another on cleaning. And we had exams in those subjects too, so we had to learn them properly. Although we went to cookery lessons, walking two miles to classes at Necton, I learned most of my cooking from my mother who was really good. She had been a head cook in London before she was married.

"After I left school at 14 I started work immediately at Dunham Farm House where the Pickering family lived. They had a big cattle farm and people used to come and buy milk from their churns, ladling it into jugs and pails. I worked there for four years and then saw a cook's job advertised at Hunstanton at a big family house called St Winifreds near the water tower. The house is still there. All supplies were delivered to the door in those days, having been ordered from local shops. I cooked regularly for the family of six. I had a half day off each week and every Sunday and I used to join a group of girls, with similar time off, and we met the lads from Burnham Market. My future husband, Dudley Franklin, was one of these Burnham lads, and we met regularly for three or four years before we married at Burnham Westgate Church on Boxing Day 1938.

"Dudley was born on 29th February 1916 – a leap year – and in between leap years we used to celebrate his birthday on 1st March. His father was a builder, and Dudley, after a time working on a farm, followed in his father's footsteps, working first for Bickells builders and then Fishers builders.

"On the day of our marriage there was deep snow. My sisters were bridesmaids but had to travel to Burnham Market by train because the roads were impassable. There was no such thing as a honeymoon for us and we moved into Number 6, Sands Cottages. This was one of the happiest communities one could ever hope for. Bucky Armiger lived at Number 1, next door to Dudley's parents. At Number 3 were the Woodhouses, some of whom married into the May family who also lived in the Cottages. 'Aunt' Harriet Woodhouse lived at Number 4 and the Parsons at Number 5. The Barbers lived next to us at Number 7 and Kathy Barber married Sands the builder. Other residents of Sands Cottages were the Fishers and the Grieves. It was a tragedy when they were scheduled for demolition in 1966 and all that community split up. We were fortunate in getting a council house at 11, Church Walk and I have lived there ever since.

"When war broke out, women with no young family had to work on the land. I worked at Sussex Farm for about three years until I had to give up because of housemaid's knee. In April 1942 ration books were issued and it was decided that all schoolchildren should be offered a cooked meal. Donald Searle, a governor of North Street Schools, offered me the job of running the proposed canteen, catering for about 100 children a day, in two sittings, boys and girls separately. The building, where Nat West Bank now stands, had been converted from the infant school and was to be used for the project. It was a hundred years old and the equipment matched its age. It was a grotty kitchen with a coal-fired cast iron range which had to be regularly blacked and polished to prevent it from rusting.

"While we had a pump for soft surface water for washing and cleaning, only after it had been boiled in large copper steamers, the drinking water had to be brought by cart from the village pump in the Market Place. This water came from a deep bore and was known as hard water. Fetching water in the water cart, a galvanised container on a two-wheeled frame with shaft handles, was a job for the older boys who could miss lessons to do this work. Recently I was talking with Brian Carter in Howells butchers shop and we were gazing out towards the site of the old Rose and Crown pub on the other side of the Market Place, reminiscing about the fun we had years ago playing darts there. I reminded Brian how he larked about when he was supposed to be delivering a cart full of water, and how I had to send him back for more when the tank arrived half empty, after all the spillage on the way.

"Bubby Middleton and I worked from 8.30 a.m to 3.30 p.m in the school kitchen. I was paid £1 per week and Bubby received 15 shillings. It was slave wages but we never thought of going on strike. We fed the children well. They had mince or sausages or a roast with potatoes and two or three vegetables, followed by steamed puddings and custard – with no lumps. It makes me cross to hear that there were lumps in the custard of school meals. There were no lumps in mine. Everything had to be mixed by hand. The children were given free milk during the morning.

"It makes me sad to see all the prepared foods the children are given today. We used to start from scratch and there was no opening of packets of bought food in my day. We cooked beef, lamb, pork and chicken from scratch and served them with freshly prepared potatoes and vegetables. We made rissoles and toad in the hole and proper puddings from the steamer. Children today are being fed a very different diet and a lot of frozen food has replaced the kitchen prepared dinners the children loved."

There are fond memories of Annie's cooking among the, now adult, pupils who fed on them. They were considered to be good, hearty food and were a positive feature of their school days. And so was Annie. She is the friendliest of souls, for whom nothing is too much trouble, and well remembered for her kindness over the years.

In September 1954 the new school in Friars Lane was opened and Annie cycled into a different world. The 20th century had arrived with a fully electrically equipped kitchen, with hot and cold water laid on. She now had four assistants catering for 250 dinners. Her skills, taught her by her mother, enabled her to adapt recipes for much larger numbers.

"I was able to be more involved with the children at Friars Lane. The assembly hall was next to the kitchen and we could hear their singing. Each day the menu was collected by one of the children to be posted on the notice board. We provided refreshments for sports day, and were cooking for the Christmas party for days leading up to the festivities. On scholarship day the pupils could choose whatever they wanted to eat for their dinner. It was usually a roast, with all the trimmings.

" The kids were pleased to come and tell us things. With Bubby (Irene) Middleton and Doris Engledown from Thorpe, we made a good team, and we got on well with a grand lot of children. I did not have one mother after me in all those years, probably because I always tried to feed the children with the food I knew they liked, rather than force them to eat food they did not like, put on the menu centrally at Norwich. I used to get permission to change menus if I knew the children would not like them. I cycled to and from Friars Lane school, sometimes returning at 8 or 8.30 at night. I never thought twice about it in those days but I should not like to do it now with the traffic as it is.

"Dudley was due to retire in 1981 and I stayed on at the school until then. They gave me a tremendous send off. I had no idea that anything was being planned, but they put on a retirement party for me, when I was presented with a rocking chair, which I sit in every day. It was lovely with all the children, and they gave me a retirement card with photographs.

"In my retirement I had planned to play bowls alongside Dudley, and we went to Fakenham to buy all the kit. He was a very keen player, and I had to buy a cabinet to keep all his silver cups he had won over the years, which were getting tarnished around the house. Together we won more trophies, but then, just three years after our retirement, he died. We had been married for 46 years and were looking forward to many more.

" I went on playing for the ladies team and was part of the team which won at county level, under our captain, Heather Emerson. I still play outdoors in the summer but, every Wednesday night in the winter, I play carpet bowls with, among others, Desmond and Margaret Ridler. I used to play darts for the British Legion ladies team but it is hard to find enough ladies now to make a team." Annie is still Secretary of the Ladies Section of the British Legion.

After she retired, Annie was approached by Dr Wright to help start a Day Centre, initially at Sutton Lea. Not only was she a founder member but she went on to cook at the Day Centre for 17 years. Annie is still Treasurer of

Burnham Market Day Centre

the WI and supports St Mary's Church as a Friend on every occasion with her cakes and teas. She has made cakes for many years for Red Cross functions, and after her retirement she became a Friend of Westgate Hall, when she and Mrs McCallum would sit and chat to the residents, to their delight. For many years she provided the teas for the Flower Show and Carnival which traditionally was the main event of the village. Her first experience of this highlight of village life was when Dudley fetched her from Hunstanton before the war. She worked with Jean Cook for the WI and still has a hand in decorating the floats.

Annie is very talented in many ways. She is an expert decorator and wall-papered all the rooms in her house. She also painted the ceilings. She makes curtains and has made some of her own clothes. Her great love is knitting and she made all Dudley's jumpers and sweaters. It is a matter of regret to her that people do not wear knitted garments so much these days but she is always willing to take on a request to make to measure. Her first interest was Fair Isle patterns using up to seven colours.

"It is such a shame that much of the village atmosphere has been lost. There were many more children in the village years ago and activities, such as dances, were held regularly, when we would meet each other in a real sense of community. The Village Hall appeal is an example of how things have changed. When we were building the present Hall the whole village joined in with enthusiasm. This time round, when we are trying to modernise it, we are finding it much harder work to raise the money, despite great efforts on the part of everyone involved."

Annie is in sparkling good health and attributes this to her years of cycling. However the fact that she is a genuinely happy person, and likes all around her to be happy too, has a lot to do with it. She never rows, or falls out with people, and is usually laughing. This does much for one's state of mind and a happy life. She radiates joy in everything she does and is completely without complaint. Whatever she is asked to do she will do with enthusiasm and there are generations in the village who have reason to be grateful to her for the service she has given – freely – over so many years. She was given some recognition for her selfless work when she received the Mayor's Civic Award for Voluntary Service during her 20 years of 'retirement'. At 87 she is an example to us all.

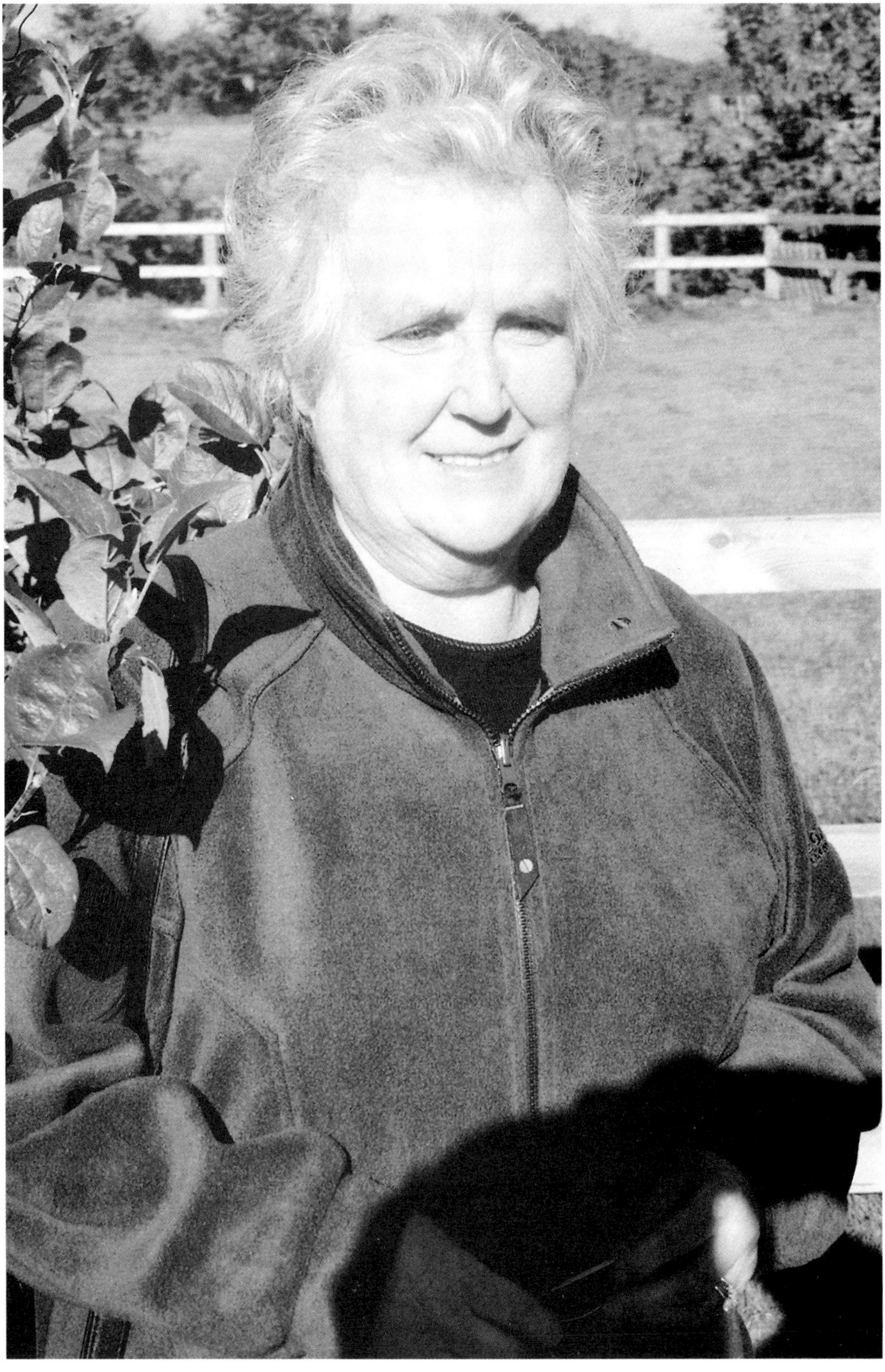

Ivy Wells

Ivy was the fourth and youngest child of Horace Arter, who was a cowman and shepherd, working for much of his career for the Roys and then for Case and Stilgoe. He met Margaret Silk from Cambridge, when she came as a maid for a Cambridge family who had a holiday home in Burnham Overy. They married in 1927. He was 21 and his bride was 20.

Horace Arter's mother, Lily, who lived in Mill Yard, was 14 when she gave birth to Horace. He was brought up by his grandmother Arter whose name he adopted. Later, Lily Arter married Bertie Mason, and their only son of that marriage was Arthur Mason. They also had two daughters, Annie and Dorothy.

When Horace and Margaret married at Sutton Church they could not afford photographs of the occasion. They lived in Mill Yard until they moved to 13 Church Walk where Jean was born and also Ivy in 1938.

Ivy remembers: "We were poor as a family, however we never lacked for food and particularly meat, which we ate in such abundance that I am sick of it today. We had a pig at the bottom of our large garden, where we grew all our own vegetables. When the pig was killed and divided into joints, it was placed in a wooden trough in the front room. The neighbours would be invited in to take a joint and, when they killed their own pigs we would have a joint from each of them. We also had lamb to eat, and game. One Christmas my father, realising there was no meat for Christmas dinner, disappeared and returned with four pheasants which he had plucked on the handlebars of his bike as he cycled home. He never did anything by halves.

"We had a rainwater tank for washing our hair, but all our household water had to be drawn in buckets, carried from the pump in Church Walk and then disposed of into a hole in the garden where the night soil went too. We had no collection service at our end of the village and no running water for any purpose in the house. On Sunday night, the big copper in the wash house would be filled by buckets, and all the flammable household rubbish burned underneath it to heat it up.

"My mother would then spend all day Monday washing and she scrubbed the kitchen table with the wash water. All day Tuesday was spent ironing. My father's white cowman's smocks had to be washed, as did the sheets, and all the other clothes in the family. If the weather was fine they were dried outside, otherwise they were draped on a line in the kitchen.

"Mrs Gladdy Roy, who eventually went blind, was very kind to us. She had four children, all about one year older than us, and would give my mother the clothes they had outgrown to be remade to fit us. My brother David, who was earning at the time, and was later to marry a widow with six children, used to give me two and sixpence a week to carry water to the house. All four children had to help out in the house. My mother, who worked hard all her life, died at 62.

"Things got better after the war when electricity and running water were laid on. During the war we would recover parachutes, if we could find them, to make into clothes and bed clothes. My father would bring home sheep skins from fallen sheep. On one occasion he swapped his overcoat for the one the Roys had put on a scarecrow because theirs was the better of the two.

"I generally disliked school, but I was always good with a needle. Miss Smith, the Headmistress, was very strict. She used to warm her backside to the fire, hitching her skirt up to the knicker legs. I left school at 15 in 1953 and went to work for Mrs Buxton at Lime Tree House. As a housemaid, I started work drawing her curtains and taking her a cup of tea at 7 a.m, and served her dinner at 6.45 p.m all for 25 shillings a week. Fifteen shillings of this went to my mother. When Mrs Buxton died I went to work for Mr Sherar who paid the same. Mrs Sherar was a great WI lady who was popular in the village. Later I worked for the Americans who paid much better.

"At the time there was a shortage of help available in the village so there was always work to do. The Americans based at Sculthorpe were renting houses in the village and would pay between one and ninepence and two and sixpence an hour.

Then there were opportunities to earn more from babysitting and David, my brother, would drive me to Sculthorpe, where there was good money to be had babysitting on the base.

"David Wells and I met in 1956 when I was 18, and he was 23, at a Labour social and dance in the North Creake village hall. That was in June and we were married in the September of the following year. David was working at Sussex Farm at the time and I was at Westgate Hall which was run by the Council as a residential home. David had spent time in the RAF to get away from home in Overy Staithe. His father was also in the RAF and seldom at home with his family of wife and five children. They were desperately poor and David's childhood was not happy. He had to make do with shoes so ill fitting that one foot is malformed to this day. He suffered from gout for many years and this, in both ankles simultaneously, is paralysingly painful.

" To relieve his childhood boredom, and develop his creativity, he and some friends went on ventures which led them into scrapes. They discovered that an airgun would shoot a half inch nail, which was not socially friendly for anyone bending down within range. He was a dab hand with a catapult and there was a time when he was implicated in the shattering of the porcelain fitments on electricity poles.

David and Ivy

"We were married at 10.30 a.m because my father had to fit it in between milking. My dress came from King's Lynn. David bought a curtain ring from John Utting's shop, to measure my finger, and went off in George Hubbard's bus to Samuels of King's Lynn to buy me an engagement ring. Having paid for the wedding service we could not afford the bells to be rung. However Nelson Moorhouse, passing by, went into the belfry and rang them for us. We had a cake from Grooms and sandwiches we had made the night before our reception at the house.

"We went to Wells by car and on to Yarmouth by train, where we spent Saturday and Sunday. We had each put a £1 note under the pillow at home to have something to spend during the week when we returned. We moved into a small flat, for which we paid 15 shillings a week, plus five shillings for electricity, in the Market Place next door to West Norfolk Radio. I was a cleaner at Westgate Hall and rose to be cook, while David was still working at Sussex Farm.

"We used to enjoy spending our days off at the beach. We would set out at 7.30 a.m for Brancaster with a loaf of bread, a piece of cheese and a jar of meat paste. We found cockles, one day, when we had nothing to put them in, so David took off his shirt and we carried them home in that. David would go to the beach at low tide, with a butt fork, to spear dabs in the pools left behind by the tide.

"When David, our son, was on the way, we moved to 9 Norton Street, Burnham Norton, in the house occupied today by Stafford and Myrtle Snell. However, at the time, the condition of that row of houses was very different. The toilet was outside and had to be emptied onto the garden. We could hear the mice scampering about above the ceiling and, when it rained, one wall ran with water inside our living room. There was no heating upstairs and I had to feed the baby downstairs, where we had a coal fire, before going upstairs to put it to bed. We had an electric cooker and we paid the Holkham Estate seven and sixpence per week rent. The Estate repaired the gable end when it all but collapsed, but did nothing inside the house. In order to make it look decent David pasted some cardboard boxes to the wall and painted over them.

"We had no car and David cycled each day to Sussex Farm. I walked to Burnham Market every other day to look after my mother, who had diabetes, and give her the necessary insulin injection. My sister looked after her on the other weekdays and my brother, David, who lived with her, took care of the week-ends. My father died aged 60.

"There were Americans renting a house just opposite us in Burnham Norton and I used to babysit for them in the evenings. Our daughter Julie was born six years after David and at last we were successful in getting a council house in Walkers Close which we later bought and where we live today. In those days the Parish Council could allocate council houses and I can remember Reg Baldry giving us the good news that we were to have one, when he called one morning on his post round. Today allocation of council houses is much more remote and the responsibility of the Borough Council.

"At last we had a flush toilet and hot and cold water laid on. I can remember my joy when we first had hot running water. I let it run out of the tap and down the sink, in celebration of this luxury. We bought a six-year-old car for £250 and David learned to drive, passing his test first time when he was 34 years old.

"David left Sussex Farm and did a bread round for Waggs for a while, until he did an egg delivery round. Then he was appointed chargehand at the CITB at Bircham Newton where for the first time he was able to contribute to a pension. In time he was declared redundant. I took every job opportunity. When David came home from work the meal was on the table and the children ready for bed and I went carrot packing at South Creake. The carrot factory was where the chocolate factory is now.

" I would come home freezing cold, but the piece work paid well and there was double pay at the weekends when they needed us. I charred in the day and packed carrots at night. We lived on David's wages and whatever I earned went towards upgrading our house and furnishings. When we first married, we had spent £200 at Aldiss on a three-piece suite, bed, wardrobe, dining table and four chairs and a sideboard. We have replaced all this three times over.

"Julie, our daughter, married Dave Watson, who used to work at Stymans, when she was 18. She now works at West Norfolk Radio and has an 18-year-old daughter Amy. Our son, David lives in Fakenham and works for Anglia Water. He has two boys, David aged 21 and Jack aged six.

"When I finished carrot packing, I found I had time on my hands in the evenings and went to Parish Council meetings to listen to them spouting. When I was declared redundant from Westgate Hall and there was a vacancy on the Parish Council, I applied along with Tom Mahon and Jeremy Thompson – who was elected to fill it. Then another vacancy occurred and I stood again, this time successfully. I have been on the Council now for nine years. It is enjoyable if you know what you are talking about.

"We get frustrated by newcomers who try to change things. However we all know the village started to die when farms went mechanical. Cottages remained empty and there were few children in the village. People who say they want it to be as it was, forget the hardships and the grind of life. I don't want to return to pumping water and emptying night soil into a hole in the garden. It is a great pity that the village became divided about the Millennium village hall.

"When Westgate Hall came onto the market, Jeremy Thompson recommended that we buy it to convert it to the village hall and playing field. It could also have been used as a conference centre and youth club. However at the time it was considered that these different uses would not go well together and the plan got no further. No doubt the debate will continue."

Dersingham

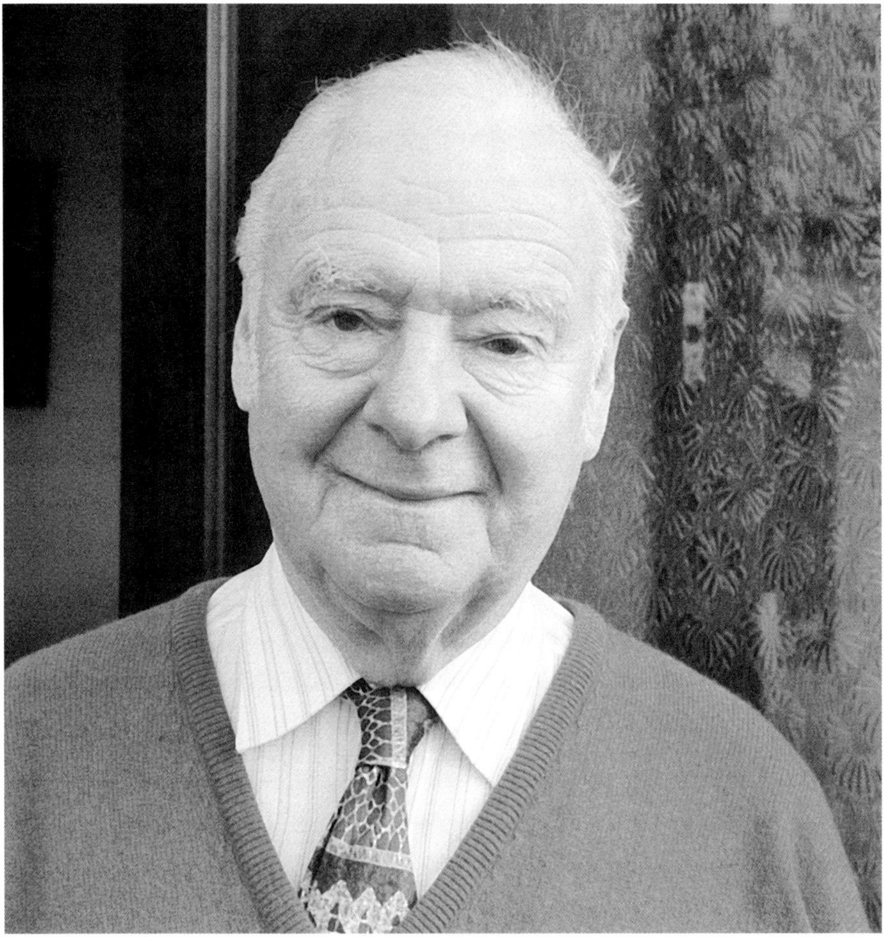

Ray Scoles

Ray Scoles and his three brothers, Billy, Philip and Peter, and their sister, Pauline, were the children of Joseph Scoles and Violet who was a Bean before she was married. The Bean family is well known in North Norfolk, notably in and around Blakeney where they joined up with the legendary Warden of Blakeney Point, Ted Eales, to form Eales and Bean to run seal boat trips to the Point – a business still carried on by their families.

"Joseph Scoles worked for many years at Roys' Mill. Born in the family cottage in Ulf Place, Burnham Market in 1924, Ray gained early experience of the butchery trade, a career in which he was destined to distinguish himself as the butcher by Royal Appointment supplying the Royals at Sandringham House from his shop at Dersingham. His brother Philip became known as the 'Bee Man'. He kept 20 or 30 hives of bees at Brancaster and sold honey and beeswax in a big way.

"Whilst still at Burnham School, I would go into Barker's butchers shop, the predecessor of Howell in Burnham Market, and sweep the floor. Sometimes I would deliver special parcels on my bike, to the villages around, starting at 7.30 in the morning and arriving at school in time for lessons at 9 a.m. I would bike to Overy to catch the tide so that Haines or Lane could deliver the meat to the beach huts. From school we would go to Wells for our carpentry lessons on a Wednesday and would stop to buy fish and chips from French's for our lunch. These were fish and chips cooked as they should be in dripping, at a price of threepence including a roll. Guineas, one of the fish and chip shops in Burnham Market, made potato fritters which were a delicious speciality.

"When I left school I went to work at Barker's as an errand boy. He would slaughter a sheep early in the morning and Mr Hancock, who supplied it and liked his sheep's kidneys fresh for his breakfast, would be one of my first deliveries. I would bike meat down to the Irish contingent, who came every summer to chop out sugar beet near Roys' Mill and they would give me a sixpence tip, which was quite a lot of money in those days for a lad on a bicycle.

"Barker had a great reputation as a slaughterman and butcher. Each week, one or two cattle, eight sheep and five pigs would go through the slaughterhouse, all bought locally from farmers who knew what the butcher and his customers expected of their meat. This daily contact was the foundation of the country butchery trade. The local butcher is still in close contact with his customers, and can still provide this service today, whereas supermarkets are much more remote from their source of supply and cannot give advice to their customers.

"Barker was one of the first butchers in the district to have a fridge, before the war. Before the use of fridges, butchers had to rely on block ice, making refrigeration less efficient and less reliable.

"Life was tough in those days and many families were struggling to make ends meet. Work was short and there were no state handouts. I used to go ferreting for rabbits with Reg Baldry to help feed the family, but also for the fun of it. When Mr Sherar cut his corn, at harvest time, as many as 30 or 40 rabbits would run out and we would help to kill them. He would then let each of us have a brace. Reggie and I also went collecting squabs – young pigeons which were, and still are, a delicacy. We would climb the trees, and take them from their nests, just as they were about to fledge. Then we would pluck them and the plump meat was delicious. I don't know why they are not on more menus today, and its not as if pigeons are in short supply. Perhaps boys don't climb trees any more.

"We would also fish for eels on the marshes, but did not use a hook to do so. We threaded sack machine twine on a needle, with a half hitch, and this would catch the eels when they took the bait. Then we would skin and boil them in milk and serve them with parsley sauce. We also reared rabbits to sell or to eat. A six-month-old rabbit would fetch sixpence and the biggest would sell for thirty shillings.

"As we got older we would play darts and dominoes in the Rose and Crown with Annie and Dudley Franklin and Fred Barber who worked for Mussets at Gallow Hill Farm for years. I was captain of the team and we played in the Massingham League. We would also play ha'penny nap with five cards. We were prepared to walk in those days, and from the age of eight or nine we walked from Sussex or Crowhall Farm to Ulf Cottages.

In that dreadful winter of 1947 Sylvia, who was later to become my first wife and who worked at Grooms, came to stay with us over the weekends. She walked to Stanhoe on a Saturday evening and back to Burnham Market again on a Sunday evening.

"Other characters in my youth were Douglas Codman who had two sisters, Evelyn and Nora. Their father was a painter and decorator and they lived in Station Road. Then there were Jack Howell who became a coalman and Herbert James, the gravedigger for Jack Williamson's undertaking business, which was situated near Harry Farrow's fish and chip shop at Ulf Place. Reggie Baldry and I both sang in the choir at Westgate Church where Joyce Curson played the organ. I was promoted from chorister to pumper of the organ. Another friend was Michael McCoy, who eventually moved to Devon and was killed when a combine fell on him. Ronnie Grint's father worked for Mrs Overman at Church End House.

"Just opposite Westgate Church was the field known as the cattle pound – now developed for housing, but still called the pound. 20 or 30 cattle would be penned there awaiting shipment by rail after sale at the cattle market each Monday – sometimes extending to Tuesday if there were too many to sell in one day. Each smallholder, of whom there were many, kept five or six cattle which they bought to fatten for the winter. They were kept in sheds, but there was a good deal of cattle driving, up and down to the marshes at Norton and Overy. When cattle were killed, Barker would hang the beast for a week, before selling the meat to his customers.

"The Flower Show was one of the highlights of the year in Burnham and was organised by Mrs Sherar. She used to invite Reggie Baldry and me up to the house for lunch on that day. I helped Fred Barber prepare his vegetables and he generally won the prizes for his exhibits. It was all on a much bigger scale then. There were trotting races, with proper carts, and lots of competitions for the children.

"I worked for Barker for many years and, when he died, I managed the shop for Mrs Barker. I lost my first wife, Sylvia, and met Jean Hamshaw again when she walked into Barker's shop one day with her Aunty May."

Jean's first husband had died aged 36 and she had three children by that marriage. She was a well known tap dancer and singer who performed at many of

Jean

the socials in the area. She had been ballet trained since the age of four and had developed as her trademark Marie Lloyd's *'My Old Man said Follow the Van'* which she performed complete with a cardboard budgie in a cage.

As she explains: " My mother was born Nora Chesney in Overy Staithe. She was a cousin of Bob Chesney, the Warden of Scolt Head for many years. When I was aged 12 and not in robust health, my Aunty May, who was married to Sam Lane and who lived in Overy, suggested that it would be better for me to come and live with her for a while rather than East Stratford in London. This was in 1939. Then war broke out and Shoreditch Central School was evacuated to Slys Farm, North Creake. I was deemed to be an evacuee and my mother joined me at Overy Staithe. The billeting officer put us into Rahere Cottage, the home of Dr Crossley-Holland opposite the Moorings Hotel. I attended Burnham Overy School from the age of 12 to 13½ and then went to the evacuated Shoreditch Central School at North Creake.

"In 1946 I returned to London and lived at home until I was married to my first husband. When he died he left me with three small children. We had been planning to buy a house in Romford but in 1962, when I had been widowed for 18 months, I had decided to move back to Norfolk. For the sake of the children, I decided that we would move to Norwich and my father, who had long wanted to return to Overy Staithe, took the opportunity to do so. So the family moved back to Norfolk. I spent nine very happy years as a secretary in the pharmacy department at the West Norwich Hospital. It was good therapy for me in that it taught me, every day, that life must go on. From the maternity to the geriatric ward the human cycle of birth to death was a reality.

"When Ray and I met up again in Barker's butchers shop we had both lost our spouses and we took up our long established friendship. He said he drove to Norwich to deliver game and I suggested he should call in for a cup of tea. He eventually did this and we were married in the following year, 1969."

Ray takes up the story: "I was a good butcher and Jean was the bookkeeper and the expert on administration. Together we made a strong team. She wanted to continue to live in Norwich so I became a town butcher for about six months, when I concluded that I much preferred being a country butcher. Barker had left me 10 acres of land up Angles Lane in Burnham Market and we decided that if I sold this and Jean sold her house we could afford to buy our own butchers shop in Dersingham which has the Royal Appointment to Sandringham House.

"Jean and I became partners in this business. However, until we had served our apprenticeship for three years to the satisfaction of the Court of the Green Cloth, which controls Royal Appointments, we had to take the Royal Warrant sign down. We passed the test and the sign went up again. For many years we have supplied Sandringham's meat orders when the Royals are in residence.

"All our cattle are bought off local farmers. We produce hams in pickle, honey and molasses, and pick out the very best for supply to Sandringham at Christmas time. We would dress the shop with pheasants and turkeys which we plucked ourselves. At one time we hung a beef carcase outside the shop on a pole. I can remember plucking 20 geese in one evening. There was some speculation, when Budgens opened in Dersingham, that it would affect our trade. But it made no difference at all. Customers who bought their meat from us continued to do so. We have a long and good relationship with them and they can get what they want in our shop.

By Royal Appointment

"When we took on the Dersingham shop in 1970 we had five children between us, aged between 10 and 18 years. In 1973 I was able, additionally, to take on the lease of Mrs High's sweet shop in Burnham Market where Humble Pie is now. I held the lease for seven years until circumstances called me back to Dersingham. In 1976 we sold the Dersingham business to Mr and Mrs Hewlitt who still run it under our name. We were able to transfer it without a further five years apprenticeship. Each year Jean, in whose name the Royal Appointment is registered and who is the only lady Royal Warrant holder in the area, and I, try to go to the Royal Warrant Holders' dinner in London where all the trades supplying the Royal Household assemble.

"I am still working in the shop and doing the work I have always enjoyed – especially the coastal rounds and seeing my old customers. Jean and I both have an interest in wildlife. I have shot pheasants for years and still go fishing at Brancaster."

Jean and Ray

The five children have all had good careers and marriages and between them have given Ray and Jean 11 grandchildren. Ray's son, Dr Graham Scoles, is the Associate Dean of Research at the College of Agriculture at the University of Saskatchewan in Canada. His daughter Lynda is married to John, a pilot at King's Lynn port. They live in Gayton.

Swaffham

Mary and Janet

Mary Tuck

Mary Tuck was born Mary Ripper in Swaffham in 1909, the third of six children – three boys and three girls in perfect alternate order. Their mother married John Thomas Ripper, a shoemaker like his father before him. She was born a Carter and was cousin to Howard Carter who discovered the Pharoah Tutankhamun's tomb with Lord Carnarvon in Egypt. The tomb was supposed to bring a curse on anyone who disturbed it and indeed Lord Carnarvon died from the effects of a mosquito bite on the cheek within months of the tomb being opened. However, Howard Carter lived on and died at the age of 65 in 1939.

Howard Carter was born in 1874, the son of Samuel John and Martha Joyce Carter of Swaffham. He was one of six children, three of whom died before he was born. His health was weak as a child, making attendance at school unwise, so he received a rudimentary education privately from local tutors. Whilst his parents had a house in Earls Court in London, it was considered better for Howard to grow up in the care of his two aunts, Fanny and Kate, who lived in a cottage on Sporle Road, Swaffham. Samuel John Carter, Howard's father, was an artist of distinction. For 20 years he was the principal animal illustrator for the *Illustrated London News* and he showed his paintings regularly at the Royal Academy's Summer Exhibition. He had an artist practice in Norfolk where he would visit the great houses and farms and paint favoured animals. One of his clients was

Sporle Road Cottage

Howard Carter

Mr Francis Allen, who lived at Cockley Cley Hall, and financed much of Howard Carter's education and his first expedition to Egypt at the age of 17 from where he progressed to become the first Chief Inspector of Antiquities in Upper Egypt. From this exalted position, Howard made an auspicious partnership as the 'learned man' at the Earl of Carnarvon's excavations, which led to the discovery of Tutankhamun's tomb. Howard Carter probably met the Allens of Cockley Cley Hall when accompanying his father on a visit and must have impressed them to receive such sponsorship.

Samuel Carter was a contemporary of Sir Edwin Landseer and is credited with the original drawings of the lions in Trafalgar Square in London, which Landseer used to produce his great sculpture at the base of Nelson's Column. The artistic talent in the family extended to Swaffhams's brightly painted carved town sign of the Pedlar of Swaffham, a 15th century local notable, John Chapman, 'who did by a dream find great treasure. This sign was carved and painted by Henry Robert (Harry) Carter, another Carter cousin of Swaffham.

There are still those about who knew Howard Carter. Benjamin Ripper, local writer, artist and hairdresser – a cousin of Howard Carter and Mary Tuck's brother – mentions Ivy Wilson who, as a little girl, ran errands for Howard Carter's mother and aunts at the Sporle Road cottage.

When Mary left school at school at 14, as one did in those days, she was apprenticed as a seamstress to Buntings departmental store in Swaffham. At the age of 16 in 1925 she met her future husband Reginald coming off a train on a day trip from Dereham where he lived. Having met Mary he was to repeat this journey many times in the years to come until eventually they married in 1931.

"I can remember waving at him as he came off the train and we became good friends. Reginald was 19 at the time and worked for International

Stores in Dereham. When we first married we lived in Watton and then Reginald was transferred to the Norwich branch when the war broke out. Reginald did duty as a fireman. Our son Malcolm was born there in 1940 and in 1943 Reginald was

Carter and Lord Carnarvon

transferred to the Burnham Market branch. We came to live in Redwins Yard, Burnham Market, between St Mary's Church and the Hoste Arms. That was 60 years ago and I have lived in Burnham Market ever since.

"Reginald stayed at International Stores until it was closed and then went to work for Allen Trailers until they too closed. After that he became a milk roundsman for Case and Stilgoe. His round was Burnham Market and the Creakes and I used to help him collect the money on a Saturday. The dairy was eventually taken over by Hood whose business was where Bruce accountants is now situated next to the Lord Nelson. When they finished in 1971, Reginald retired.

"I used to fix the blackout at the house in Norwich and this included blocking the keyhole. It was so dark, entering the house, I am surprised we did not break our legs falling over the furniture. I can remember the air raids in the First World War when as a little girl in Swaffham I sat under a big round table until that was thought to be too little protection. We then went to the cellar of a big house next door. Later on we had a shelter in the garden. We would drink tea and listen to the sound of the 'angels in the sky' as I called them, although their purpose was anything but angelic."

One of Mary's talents was bowls. "Until quite recently ladies were not allowed to join the men's bowls club so we started our own behind the Hoste and three of us became good enough to play for Norfolk. There was Audrey Radcliffe and Vi High and me. We made up a block (team) and I was the 'skip' which meant I bowled last. This was a responsible position as the objective was to knock our opponents' woods away from the jack and leave our own alone, or nudge them nearer. We were very smart in our white skirts and blue blazers.

"Reginald also played bowls, particularly after he retired in 1971 until about 1980. He had a stroke and was nearly 90 when he died. It was all very sad, and mainly unexpected, because he was generally in good health."

Mary has kept up her sewing over the years, making alterations to clothes. "I did a lot of sewing for Dr Woodsend, a doctor in Burnham Market for many years, and I find it gives me something to do when I am sitting doing nothing else. I never could sit without activity.

"As children we all knew of Harry Carter's town sign at Swaffham and the dream of the Great Treasure. I imagined the Great Treasure was ice cream. We used to get up to some pranks as children. A favourite was to hollow out an orange and leave it in the road to look as if it was whole and juicy. Then we would watch the attention it drew and eventually someone picked it up and carried it away, only to find that it was a hollow skin. We would also knock on a row of front doors on our way back from church and then rapidly turn round and retrace our steps, so that it looked as if we were coming from the other direction and therefore quite innocent."

Mary's son Malcolm works as a butcher for Arthur Howell in Burnham Market where he is a well known character. He worked for Waggs baker from 1963 to 1967 and then started work for Mrs Barker whose butchers shop was bought by Arthur Howell in 1971. He left in 1988 but returned three years ago. He is the one with the daffodil in his hat. In 1963 he married Janet – the ever popular and dependable Janet – who has worked at Burnham Stores for the last seven years. Before that she worked at the Lord Nelson for eight years for Peter Jordan, the well known mushroom expert and before that, for 10 years at Ulf Drapery where Gillies is now. That business was started by Ernie Utting in 1963.

Mary, now 93, enjoys the Day Centre in North Street and remembers the old days. For example, Alice Adora Hubbard, whose ability to sell raffle tickets for good causes and persuade all who tried to pass her in the street to buy, is still etched in the memory. She also recalls the days long ago when she and Reginald had dancing lessons in the old village hall from Mr Starling, the AA man.

Wells-next-the-Sea

Arthur and Freda

Arthur Howell

In 1889 Arthur Howell, who was working for Purdy's butchers in Binham, decided to start a business of his own. He opened his first butchers shop in Binham Westgate, buying his meat, initially, from other butchers and delivering orders in the district. Later he moved his business to the present

Old shop

shop in Binham. His son, John Robert Howell, born in 1890, worked with his father from the early 1900s. He had five children: Arthur, the eldest who was born in 1920 and, at the age of 82, still puts in a full working day; John, who ran the Staithe Street shop in Wells after his father had bought it in the 1940s; Archie and his sister Margaret who ran the Binham shop, abattoir and smokery; and Dennis who ran the family 30-acre farm at Binham.

John Robert Howell had a brother, William, whose family run that amazing hardware shop in Binham. Its capacity to find even the most obscure item for a customer has spread its reputation well beyond Binham. It has developed further into a supermarket and is run by William's two sons, Trevor and Kenny. Another son, Raymond, has greenhouses.

Arthur Howell was born in Woodsend, Binham. His parents could not get the accommodation over the shop because it was occupied by tenants.

Binham shop

He recalls: "I went to school, first at Binham and then at Wells, where I can remember my teachers. The Head, at the time, was Mr Ashton and there was Mr Monckton and Mr Leader. I was not a particularly remarkable student and had little interest in games. I had absolutely no interest in the sea and have never been in it or on it to this day.

"I joined my father in the business on leaving school at the age of 14 in 1934, delivering orders in all weathers, from a bicycle with a frame and basket in the front – like Granville in *Open All Hours.* Another parallel with this much later TV show was that my father also had a till which, when he pulled the handle, would shoot out with force and clatter. It was well not to be in the direct line of fire. My round took me through the villages of Warham, Wighton, Wells and Stiffkey. Then my father bought me a horse van. In fact I had two horses. One did the round on Tuesdays and Fridays and the other Wednesdays and Saturdays. It was too much for one horse to work it every day. When I was 17, I learned to drive a motor van and passed my test in King's Lynn first time.

"During my round I got to know my customers and their families. This is how Freda and I first met. We married during 72-hour army leave in 1941 and celebrated our diamond wedding in 2001. Freda's father and mine were friends and it was logical that I should dally when delivering meat to their home. The horse knew it would be a long call, and pulled well into the side of the road whenever we arrived at their house. My father was a good businessman. He would buy cattle in Fakenham market or from local farmers, if they had beasts of the right quality, and drive them to Binham and later to Wells where a second abattoir was built. He would slaughter them himself and built up the business's reputation.

"In 1941, at the age of 20, I was called up into the army and joined the Royal Artillery. This was not my first choice for, as a Norfolk butcher, I would have preferred the Royal Norfolk Regiment or, as it happened later, the Army Catering Corps where I could use my skills. I was posted to Leeds for six to eight weeks, located at anti aircraft gun sites, and then to Huddersfield where ICI had a big installation. Then we went to protect the Sunderland docks which the enemy bombed heavily. However, they had the measure of our tracer shell range and stayed just above it out of harm's way while they rained bombs on us. In the six months I spent in that hostile environment I was spared injury.

"In preparation for D Day we were posted to Hove, where we spent 18 months in total, before and after D Day. The amount of equipment collected in the area was staggering. Had we been able to land it all, as planned, in France, the Allies would have been unstoppable. As we know, eventually they were, but it was a very tough struggle to get the momentum established with the practical problems encountered on landing in France. I remember the huge 'cotton reels' being unwound across the Channel carrying fuel pipes and electric wires. The sky was black with Allied planes. On the night before D Day a despatch rider arrived with a sealed envelope for each commanding officer with instructions that it was not to be opened before midnight. The invasion troops moved out at 3 a.m.

"In 1942 I had been transferred to the Army Catering Corps and later moved to Ashton under Lyme to prepare the huge demob centre there for the rush to come. I spent my time in the stores, butchery and cookhouse. I was demobbed in 1946 and returned to Binham. Whilst I was away, my father had bought the Staithe Street shop and my brother John, who was medically unfit for the army, was running it. I spent my time half at Wells and half at Binham. We were all in the business until Father died in 1956. The arrangement he left was that John and I would have the Wells shop, Archie and Margaret the Binham shop, and Denny the farm.

"Archie got married and he and Margaret decided they wanted to leave the business if John and I would buy them out – which we did. John then took over the Binham shop for three or four years until he too decided to do something else with his life and I bought him out. So from 1959 I was in charge of the business. In 1964 I bought out Rams butchers in the High Street and our daughter Gloria set up her first hat shop in the front room

Winning team

of the house that used to be the butchers shop. We continued to expand. I bought the business, but not the property of the Walsingham shop, and when Dewhurst wanted to sell their shop in Wells in the early 1990s, on the other side of Staithe Street, I bought that.

" In 1971 Mrs Barker, who with her husband owned the butchers shop in Burnham Market, and continued to run it after his death, asked me if I wanted to buy the business. It had a very strong reputation and I bought it and Pentney House next door where Mrs Barker continued to live, undisturbed, until her death. Then Gloria moved her hat shop into it and expanded the business. I later bought the Present House in Wells which is now also owned and run by Gloria." Pentney House Hats has a widespread reputation. Customers come from all over the country to buy their hats, from a choice of 5000, for their special occasions. It is reputed to be the largest hat shop in Britain.

"I had always been interested in a piece of farm land between Binham and Wells, having cycled passed it many a time in my early days, and not least because it has associations with my

Present House

courting days with Freda. In 1990, when I was 70 years old, it came on the market and I bought the 60-acre Fiddlers Hill Farm from the Council." There is an ancient story – some would say myth - about the origin of the name, Fiddlers Hill. In 1499 a tramp with his dog heard that there was a tunnel between Binham Priory and Walsingham Abbey. He offered to investigate. He entered the tunnel playing his violin and said he would play all the way through it, so the village could hear how far the tunnel extended.

Pentney House

Then the music suddenly stopped. In 1933 during a road widening scheme, the skeletons of a man and a dog were unearthed.

Freda's family, the Halls, have lived in Wells for three generations since her gypsy ancestors came there from Lincolnshire. Her father was the farmer at Orchard Farm and her mother's father a coal merchant. In 1940 John Robert Howell asked Freda to come to his butchers shop and do the books for 15 shillings a week. She has worked in the business continually ever since.

"The centre of Wells has moved from the High Street to Staithe Street," says Freda. "While the railway was operating, people would walk from the station along Marsh Lane, which connected it with the High Street. But the shops in the High Street gradually closed and shoppers use Staithe Street today. The Quay has more to do

Former butchers shop in High Street, Wells

with holiday makers and trippers today than with fishing, which was its traditional focus, and this has helped to pull the shops towards it.

"We started our own Bowls Club during 1970s/80s for our staff. We joined the North Norfolk League and won the Grange Cup one year. For many years we held an annual staff dinner and dance at the Victoria Hotel Holkham and, at Christmas and for the carnival and regatta in the summer, we would trim up our shops. We would work all Friday night until the early hours of Saturday morning and nearly always won first or second prize. Arthur would go to King's Lynn market at Christmas and buy prize animals. We would display the meat with its winning rosettes. Each winter we have a selection of local game and venison from the Holkham estate. We had approximately nine delivery vans on the road and would enter one in the carnival every year and invariably won a prize."

Freda has a wealth of stories about Wells and its characters. Some of this is set down in her book of poems which she reads to WI and other gatherings. For example, the story of the Ratting Competition in Wells has been committed to poetry. The town was invaded by a plague of rats in 1933/34 and the council set up a bounty scheme to pay a ha'penny a tail to eliminate them. The rats invaded all parts of the town including *Our dear old Buttlands*. This campaign was a welcome distraction to young Freda who wrote:- *(three extracts from her 17 verse poem)*

> *Now I should have been doing my homework*
> *All ready for school next day,*
> *But every night as they started out*
> *I was with them on their way*
>
> *Around my neck they hung a lamp*
> *It came, I think, from a car,*
> *It was one of those great old carbide things*
> *And my heart it had some power*
>
> *When we got the most that we could catch*
> *We returned to a good night's sleep,*
> *To dream we were still wandering*
> *Among cattle all asleep*

She also recalls some old Wells characters including Bertie Edwards whose wife had left him and moved to Warham. He followed her and took up residence in the house next door. He was a shortsighted man whose eyesight seemed to make a remarkable recovery if someone filled his beer glass. He would wear a top hat with a 'sparrow tail coat' and old brown plus-fours or an old fur coat with a bowler hat with a rose stuck into, or hunting pink. The more outrageous his clothes the more drinks they would buy him in the pub and persuade him to sing his party piece, 'The *Old Kitchen Kettle*'. *(Extract verse from Freda's 15 verse poem):-*

> *He had large, thick, bushy eyebrows*
> *And a chin quite near his nose,*
> *His legs were bowed. His hands were gnarled,*
> *In fact, he matched his clothes*

Arthur and Freda's son Arthur has taken on the family tradition and runs the business. It is still very much a family affair with Freda in the Staithe shop, taking orders by phone from the hotels and restaurants who call at all hours for next day delivery, and from private customers who have been loyal to Howell butchers for a lifetime. She knows many of her customers well and there is never any shortage of chat and memories when she is present at the Staithe

Arthur Howell Jnr

Street shop. Arthur Senior, who says of himself that he is the errand boy these days, delivers meat to his shops and local catering establishments, when he is not serving behind the counter at one of them.

Arthur Jnr is married to Liz, who manages the holiday cottages in Binham and does the administration for the business. They have a daughter – so has Gloria and her husband, and a grandson. Arthur Jnr and his family have recently moved into Angus House in the High Street, while his parents have moved into a smaller and more convenient house nearby.

Arthur Snr and Freda have only had one holiday in all their 61 years of marriage. They have a 20-year-old Rolls Royce and belong to the RR Association. The 10-day holiday was organised by the Association when 86 Rolls Royces toured Scotland, staying in Stakis hotels. While both enjoyed the holiday, neither is in any hurry to have another one. Work is their business. Arthur Snr starts at 7.30 a.m, breaks off for lunch, and returns to work in the afternoon until 5.30 or 6 p.m. The shop is open on Sunday mornings too. His dedication to the business has left little time for

Staithe Street, Wells

involvement in other activities although, for some years, he was President of the Men's Institute in Wells.

The success of this family butchery business over 113 years is remarkable in the light of the decline of small shops in general and butchers in particular. However, Arthur Howell has retained the link between its customers and the farmers who supply local meat to its specifications. This is unusual in the age of detached and impersonal supermarkets. Most customers like to chat while they shop, and get good meat and good advice. The latter is unlikely at the supermarket check-out, whilst it is a certainty in a Howell shop. Furthermore the staff in the shop have, for the most part, been there for decades. Maurice Bailey, who retired after 51 years, was the longest serving, but others are not far behind. Arthur Howell represents not only reassuring quality, but continuity in an uncertain age.